WRITING *as a* SACRED PATH

A Practical Guide to Writing with Passion and Purpose

JILL JEPSON

CELESTIAL ARTS
Berkeley | Toronto

CA

Celestial Arts
an imprint of Ten Speed Press
PO Box 7123
Berkeley, California 94707
www.tenspeed.com

Distributed in Australia by Simon and Schuster Australia, in Canada by Ten Speed Press Canada, in New Zealand by Southern Publishers Group, in South Africa by Real Books, and in the United Kingdom and Europe by Publishers Group UK.

Cover and text design by Katy Brown

Library of Congress Cataloging-in-Publication Data
Jepson, Jill Christine, 1950–
    Writing as a sacred path : a practical guide to writing with passion and purpose / Jill Jepson.
        p. cm.
    Includes bibliographical references and index.
    Summary: "A guide to approaching creative writing as a sacred art, including writing exercises, prompts, and strategies inspired by diverse spiritual traditions and practices"—Provided by publisher.
        ISBN-13: 978-1-58761-325-8
        ISBN-10: 1-58761-325-5
    1. Creative writing—Religious aspects. I. Title.
    PN171.R45J46 2008
    801—dc22

                                        2008021952

Printed in the United States of America
First printing, 2008

1 2 3 4 5 6 7 8 9 10 — 12 11 10 09 08

For my father

Contents

Acknowledgments

This book rests on the work of many. To all of them, I offer my thanks: to my brilliant editor, Kyra Ryan, for her help in honing an unwieldy collection of chapters into a focused manuscript; to Brie Mazurek and Julie Bennett at Ten Speed Press for the clarity and expertise they have brought to this book; and to my agent, Winifred Golden, for her wisdom and hard work throughout the process of bringing this book into print.

I am profoundly grateful to my parents, Irene and Clifford Jepson, for their unwavering devotion and love; to the many friends and family who have supported my writing over the years, including Lynette Brasfield, Karen Pliskin, Jennifer Jepson, and Tom and Chris Jepson. Special thanks goes to Kristina Santos, whose kindness has sustained me through the trials of the writing life, and to Eleanor Burian-Mohr for her unreserved friendship, immense generosity, and practical assistance. I also thank Pixie, Winona, and Durango for their uncomplicated, steadfast trust.

Finally, my deepest gratitude goes to my husband John, the love of my life.

{1}

The Call

IF YOU ARE READING THIS BOOK, you have already heard the call. Maybe, at this point, it's just a whisper, a small voice quietly urging you to put your ideas down in words. It occurs to you that you might try writing some day. You think, "I should write the story of my grandmother's life" or "If only I could create a poem about the way my kitchen smells in the morning."

Or perhaps the voice is more insistent. Characters appear full-blown in your consciousness, complete with faces and bodies, histories and dreams. It isn't so much that you've thought the characters up as that they have arrived uninvited. You wake up to find them sitting at the foot of your bed saying, "Well? Have you given us substance yet?" You long to put it all down on paper. You have to tell their stories.

Here is a shocking truth: few people write because it is fun. It can be fun, even exhilarating and delightful, but that's not why writers write. True writers keep at it even when the experience falls squarely between aggravating and ghastly. They labor at work that sometimes depresses and exhausts them, for little pay (or none at all), even in the face of failure. This impulse may sound like masochism or addiction, and perhaps it is, but it is also something greater and more compelling: it's a vocation, a calling.

In the spiritual sense, a vocation is not merely a job one sets out to do, but an irresistible impulse, an urge strong enough to lead a man or woman to renounce a successful career for a life of service, to give up children and family for the rigors of the monastery—or to risk everything in order to write. Like religious men and women, writers often feel they've been chosen or destined for their work. Novelist Starling Lawrence describes his desire to write as a "commanding impulse."[1] Arthur Conan Doyle, Sherlock Holmes's prolific creator, saw his writing as something "marked out" for him by Providence.[2] "I write because I can't *not write* any more than I could *not breathe*," says novelist Elaine Marie Alphin.[3] Writing isn't something you choose to do, in the way you might decide to become a teacher or firefighter. More often, writing chooses you.

Answering the call to write is not easy. It's not convenient to discover that you will need to spend a significant portion of your time doing hard, often unrewarded labor, much of which may end up moldering unpublished in your file cabinet of sorrows. It throws an oversized monkey wrench into your financial situation, your family life, and your romantic relationships—and the material rewards are often elusive.

Responding to the call to write, as with following any true vocation, requires a kind of surrender—a yielding that can be painful and frightening. It takes the courage to forge ahead even when you have no idea where you're going. It takes a willingness to accept the possibility of failure. It means relinquishing a certain amount of control over your life for the sake of something larger. These challenges have driven many a writer to drink and many others to business school. But the profound satisfaction you will draw from writing is worth every minute of doubt and fear.

Despite its inconveniences and frustrations, the compelling nature of the writing life has some enormous benefits. People with vocations are frequently praised for their commitment by those who agree with them and depicted as zealots by those who don't. Both responses are due to their immense stores of energy, dedication, and persistence. Writers are no exception. It is the call to write that provides us with the internal resources we need—the vigor and tenacity, the ability to juggle time and commitments, the skill at screening out external distractions and internal noise. The call gives you the stamina and strength you need to keep from falling by the wayside. For writers who find themselves stuck in the terrible no-man's-land of writer's block, that sense of being called can provide the courage to stick with their writing until the floodgates open. The vocation gives you the ability to find a way, no matter what kinds of barriers loom ahead of you.

Legend has it that when St. Perpetua, a third-century Christian martyr, was asked to renounce her faith, she responded by gesturing to a vase. "Could it be called by any other name than what it is?" she asked. "Well, so too, I cannot be called anything other than what I am."[4] The factual accuracy of this story is debatable, but the truth it conveys is right on target: Perpetua was not merely following a path; she *was* the path.

Writers know this feeling well. When you write regularly, it becomes such a fundamental part of the way you live that you cannot conceive of your life without it. At some point, you discover you are unable to separate yourself from the act of writing or think about yourself other than as a writer. Novelist and short-story writer William Goyen describes it as, "a way to observe the world and to move through life, among human beings."[5] When you are called, writing is more than something you do, it is what you are.

Noble laureate Toni Morrison has said that in order to weed out the overwhelming number of commitments she faced, she had to ask herself which were the things she absolutely had to do—the things without which, she would die. She had two: her family and her writing. Many writers share the feeling that writing is what keeps them alive. Sometimes, they mean this quite literally. Poet Frank O'Hara said that the one thing that kept him from suicide was the thought that, if he died, he would never write another poem. And Pamela Wagner, a poet who suffers from schizophrenia, says that it is writing that has kept her alive—in every sense of the word. Even if writing isn't the one thing that stands between you and madness or suicide, it is what makes a writer *feel* alive. If you are called to the path, not following it is a kind of living death. Writing is as natural and as necessary as breathing.

When we speak of writing as a spiritual vocation, one concern that naturally arises is its relationship with other aspects of your spiritual life. For many, writing itself can be the essence of spirituality: it may encompass the beliefs and practices that lie at the core of your spiritual path. But if you are already committed to a particular set of practices and beliefs, how does writing fit in? Does it detract from your faith? What role can it play?

To speak of writing as a spiritual vocation does not necessarily mean that it should or will take the place of other aspects of your spirituality. In fact, your writing can serve your spiritual life, whatever path you are on. It can nourish your beliefs, deepen your awareness, and strengthen your conviction. It can bring your values into focus, clarifying and energizing your way along your chosen path. Of course, overtly sacred writing—like keeping a spiritual journal or writing sacred poetry—can support your practice, but writing can serve your spiritual life even if it isn't explicitly sacred. Anything that is written with authenticity—whether a serious essay or a comedy sketch—gives you the opportunity to examine your relationship to the human community, the Earth, and the Divine. That examination goes right to the core of your spirituality.

If your path is largely devotional, writing can be a form of prayer. This is true whether you view prayer as a way of asking God for something or as a subtler act of communing with the sacred, showing gratitude to the Universe or, as St. John of Damascus put it fourteen centuries ago, "lifting up the mind" to the Divine.[6] Poet Patrice Vecchione, author of *Writing and the Spiritual Life*, says that every time a person sits down to write, he is "asking for language,"[7] which is in itself an act of prayer. Furthermore, when we write, we are showing a deep appreciation for the world around us and for our opportunity to journey through it as human beings. The stories and poems we create are offerings of gratitude for those gifts. The Trappist monk Thomas Merton didn't consider writing to be a form of prayer, but said it helped him pray because it made the "mirror inside" very clear: "God shines there and is immediately found, without hunting, as if he had come close to me while I was writing, and I had not observed his coming."[8]

For those whose paths are more contemplative than devotional, writing can also serve as a form of meditation. Theosophical thinker Helen V. Zahara defined meditation as "a technique of self-exploration" that entails "the opening of one's heart and the turning of one's mind in new directions. . . ."[9] Writing involves the same self-exploration, open heart, and willingness to think in new ways. It also requires the same type of deep, focused attention that meditation entails. Poet Naomi Shihab Nye, for example, compares the "long, loving look that we use when we write" to the continuous, deep looking at reality we do during meditation.[10]

Writing can also be an integral part of your practice if your spiritual path is focused on doing good work in the world. To write in service of a good cause is to offer the world a great and powerful gift. Few forms of charity are as profound and long lasting as that of the writer who exposes social injustices and encourages others to do good works. This writing doesn't have to come in the form of hard-hitting journalism or essays: a work of fiction or poetry can enlighten people about the need for social change and motivate them to act.

Writing can nourish your spiritual life regardless of whether you are committed to a particular practice or faith. For those who are seeking a path, it can serve as a guide for the search and as a companion while you seek—and might end up being the path you are looking for. If you find talk of spirituality off-putting, know that writing can serve many of the functions of spiritual paths—as an expression of gratitude or love, as a connection with the world, and as a union with something greater than oneself—without the requirement that you adhere to particular beliefs or rituals.

Regardless of how you view the role of writing in your spiritual life—whether it is a companion to other spiritual practices, one of a set of practices, or the very essence of your spirituality—developing the sacred aspects of writing can create a remarkable synergy. Bringing your own personal sense of the sacred to your writing can give your work the power of conviction and infuse it with surprising creativity. When you see your writing as more than a hobby, profession, or craft—as a profound expression of your self—you have no choice but to write with utter conviction and authenticity. The deepest sources of creativity within you will open.

This book came from just that kind of synergy, from the coming together of two streams that had been flowing through my life for decades. On the one hand, it grew from my many years of exploring, studying, and experimenting with spiritual practices throughout the world. That search took me from Siberia to Syria, Nepal to Guatemala, and many places in between. I studied the traditions of every faith I encountered, and interviewed scores of lay people, monastics, and clergy, including Central American shamans, Tibetan Buddhist nuns, Sikh gurus in India, Shinto priests in Japan, and Hindu holy men in the Himalayas. I also visited households of ordinary people—Muslims, Orthodox Jews, Quakers, Hindus, and others—to see how they worshipped. I studied their sacred texts, learned about their rituals, and delved into their philosophies.

I also wrote—incessantly and rather compulsively—from the time I was a very young child. That was the second stream from which this book grew. Oddly, I wrote for many years without seeing the connection between my writing and my spiritual search. But as both of these facets of my life matured, I gradually became aware that the things I found in writing were the same things others sought in ritual, prayer, and meditation—in all the various practices and traditions of their faiths. I soon found I was not the only writer who felt this way. In biographies, interviews, essays, and letters, writers from many eras and all over the globe speak of writing in the same terms used by practitioners of spiritual traditions. They tell of transcendence, connection with the Universe, a sense of purpose and meaning. Many of them use the terms *sacred* and *divine*; many speak of being in touch with something greater than themselves.

Using the insights of these writers, my own experiences, and the knowledge I had gained from my writing students, I began developing spiritual workshops and serving as a spiritual coach for writers. After several years of working with small groups and individual writers, I knew I needed to bring the ideas, observations, activities, and exercises I had developed to a larger audience. This book is a result of that effort.

In this book, you will find ideas, suggestions, and activities to deepen your writing and aid you on your spiritual journey. Each chapter provides tools designed to offer encouragement and guidance along the sacred path of the writer. Each explores new ways to think about writing and draws a wealth of knowledge from both spiritual traditions and the experiences of writers past and present to aid in the development of each person's own personal, true, and authentic spiritual path.

Because spirituality is such a vast topic, I have organized this book around four paths or gateways to the sacred: those of the mystic, the monk, the shaman, and the warrior. Each of these paths is a distinct approach to the Divine; each shows striking parallels with the writing life; and each offers a unique set of insights for writers. In part I, "The Mystic Journey," we will explore the heightened awareness and intuitive understanding reached by mystics from traditions throughout the world. We will look at the mystic's experience of transcending the boundaries of the ego, being in touch with higher powers, and achieving a sense of oneness with the All. We will examine the mystic's "crazy wisdom"—that unique ability to break out of everyday thinking and see reality in a new light. We will look at the ways writers also go beyond themselves, discuss ideas and suggestions for opening ourselves to alternate ways of viewing the world, and show how, at the height of creativity, a writer can enter a kind of consciousness remarkably similar to that of the mystic.

Part II, "The Monastic Path," explores the simple contemplative path of the monk, focusing on two essential and complementary aspects of the monastic experience: solitude and community. We will look first at the role of silence and solitude in the life of the monk and the writer, at what gifts and challenges they offer, and at ways to cultivate them in our busy lives. But the monastic life is not only one of silent work and contemplation: it rests on close-knit communities working together. "The Monastic Path" asks what monks can teach us about working harmoniously with others and examines the profound, often overlooked, importance of community in the writing life.

In part III, "The Way of the Shaman," we will explore the shamanic voyage into the spirit world and the striking parallels between that voyage and the writer's journey into the subconscious. Part III will draw on shamanic knowledge to explore ways writers can expand their consciousness, fearlessly explore their deepest memories, and enter new realms of imagination. It will use the shaman's wisdom to show how we can face our metaphorical spirits—both evil and benevolent—and learn from them. We will also look at the shaman's intimate relationship with the natural world, the years she spends living in and learning from nature, and the plant and animal teachers from whom she gains wisdom. Part III delves into the ways that an intimate relationship with the Earth serves as a source of shamanic power. It offers techniques for writers to deepen their own relationships with natural places, the plant world, and our nonhuman kin.

Part IV, "The Warrior Road," examines the courage, fortitude, and valor that constitute the sacred code of the honorable warrior. It shows that the writer's path requires the same sort of strength, sureness, and bravery that the warrior needs on the battlefield. It will suggest ways writers can develop those essential qualities by learning from the focus, discipline, and strategic skill that lies at the heart of the warrior's training.

The chapters in this book look at the philosophies and beliefs central to these four gateways to the sacred, but each chapter focuses on specific Sacred Tools—exercises, activities, prompts, and ideas for incorporating the wisdom of each path into your writing life. These Sacred Tools offer ways to ignite your creativity, dissolve blocks, delve more deeply into memory and imagination, transform negative feelings such as fear and disappointment, and open yourself to fresh awareness. They include visualizations, journaling, poetry writing, and meditations. Some offer prompts to stimulate ideas for writing. Others incorporate simple crafts, nature activities, observation exercises, and interactions with those around you. You may approach the tools any way you like. Do them each one by one or seek out the ones that especially call to you. Do them once or many times, or make them a regular part of your writing life. Of course, you are free to alter any of them to suit your own spiritual search.

Writing as a Sacred Path offers ways for you to come to a deeper, richer relationship with your writing—and with yourself. It provides a springboard to a new level of skill and confidence and a gateway to greater power and authenticity in your writing. It offers a new way of thinking about your writing and your life as a writer. Explore, experiment, and have fun. Allow yourself to go wherever the call to write leads you.

The Sacred Gift

ALL WRITERS, be they novelists, poets, journalists, or scholars, are, at root, tellers of tales, and it is in their role as storytellers that the sacred core of writing lies. Despite our impulse to search what we read for themes, symbols, metaphors, "what the author is trying to say," and such, it is in the act of storytelling that writers perform their cardinal work.

Storytelling may seem too commonplace—even trivial—to be the key to a writer's spiritual path. But this is because, like all seemingly simple work, we have become so used to it that we fail to see how remarkable it is, and how strange. When you try to analyze the feat of telling a story, it becomes an act of immense complexity and depth.

When you tell a story, you become what F. Scott Fitzgerald called "part of the consciousness of our race."[1] Storytellers are the custodians of human history, the recorders of the human experience, the voice of the human soul. They are the ones who keep safe the vast store of information collected by the human race over time. Perhaps this is what E. B. White meant when he wrote in "The Ring of Time": "As a writing man, or secretary, I have always felt charged with the safekeeping of all unexpected items of worldly or unworldly enchantment, as though I might be held personally responsible if even a small one were to be lost."[2]

But storytelling does more than record and transmit human experience—it also gives form to that experience. Stories sculpt meaning; they shape how we think about the world; they provide the framework for understanding our place in the Universe. Stories determine what we cherish, despise, or ignore. They define, in fact, what it is to be human.

According to a (possibly apocryphal) story, when Martha Graham was once asked to explain what one of her dances meant, she said, "If I could say it, I wouldn't have to dance it." Stories function the same way: They express the inexpressible. They take the vast, transcendent, and ineffable and make it small and concrete enough to talk about. We may not be able to understand the spark of divinity that lies within us, but we can understand a story about a man who was at once human and the son of God. We have no way to express the truth that, though we are bound to die, our substance continues to live as part of the Universe, but we have myriad tales of beings who have transcended death. We struggle with the concepts of good and evil, but we can tell stories, as Hindus do, about deities who contain both creation and destruction within them. As Anaïs Nin put it, we tell stories, "not to say what we can all say, but what we are unable to say."[3]

Finally, stories remind us that we are not separate, isolated individuals afloat in the cosmos, but part of the universal stream of life. When we read a story, we leave our individual selves behind and become one with the characters whose lives we see played out. We become aware on some primitive level that we are not disconnected, solitary beings, but part of the chain of life that goes back to the first appearance of a living cell and continues indefinitely into the future.

Stories are gifts. The Universe offers them, not merely to us as individual writers, but to the world. Writers are the ones charged with the work of giving stories form and passing them on to others. To receive and be open to stories, to receive them, to treat them with care and respect, and to offer them to the world is not merely our work, but our sacred responsibility.

INVITING AND RECEIVING STORIES

"Whatever way your stories come to you is the right way,"[4] says children's author R. L. LaFevers. Her choice of words is important: she isn't talking about building, creating, or even discovering stories, but about stories *coming to us*. Rather than going out to hunt for them, we must be open and receptive to stories. We have to wait for them, sometimes with immense patience. But this does not mean that there is nothing we can do but stare out the window wishing for inspiration. In fact, we must be alert, pay attention, and be ready to receive stories when they come. There are many things we can do to be sure we are open to the arrival of stories.

───────────────{ SACRED TOOL }───────────────

Receiving Stories from Everyday Life

We do not have to go to the ends of the Earth or have life-changing adventures to find material. Stories are everywhere, from Himalayan peaks to your dentist's office. In fact, the richest source of stories isn't the dramatic event that comes once in a decade, but the ordinary workings of daily life.

The key to finding stories in everyday experiences—or anywhere, for that matter—is the realization that we are not searching for fully fleshed-out ideas complete with characters, settings, and plots. Instead, we are keeping our eyes open to the story potential in day-to-day events. Unless we are journalists doing reportage, our task is not to sit down and replicate an event exactly. Rather, we find the core of the experience—that part of the event that makes it compelling—and use our imaginations to create stories from it. Here is how it is done:

1. *Reflect.* At the end of the day, sit down, close your eyes, and think about what has happened since you woke up. Most of the time, the various conversations and activities will seem pretty commonplace. That doesn't matter: pick one and focus on it. Perhaps you had a discussion with your boss about a difficult client. Maybe your second grader came home delighted at praise she'd received from a teacher. Maybe you had to shop in a crowded supermarket when you were tired and headachy after work. Whatever you pick, quietly review the incident in your mind. Don't just mentally list what happened— relive it. Picture yourself stepping into your boss's office or first seeing the look on your child's face. Delve into the sensory aspects of your experience, recalling what you saw, heard, felt, smelled, and tasted during the event.

2. *Consider the details.* Once you have fully immersed yourself in the memory of the event, explore its particulars:

    ✦ Who were the major characters in this episode? Who else was present? Who was most involved? In the supermarket, for example, characters might include the guy who bumped into you in a rush to get to the dairy case or the clerk who chatted with you cheerfully.

    ✦ Don't forget yourself. In some cases, you will be the main character—maybe even the only character. In others, you may fade into the background, becoming the narrator of a story you observed.

    ✦ Remember the minor characters. In addition to the speed demon with a shopping cart, there is the passerby who glanced at you when you got bumped. Along with the cheerful supermarket clerk, there are the two noisy teenagers in line behind you.

3. *Identify each person's needs.* What did each of these characters want? Everyone always has something they hope to accomplish, whether it is to solve some problem, get some important (or trivial) work done, or just relax. Here is where we begin to diverge from the actual event into the world of story-making. We don't really know what any of these people thought or felt. Remember: we are not trying to report on an event but to use that event as the core of a story.

   For each character in the story, there is a wealth of possible needs and desires. The guy who ran into you in the produce aisle might be trying to get home to a sick child—or he might be someone who goes through life with a sense of entitlement and a chip on his shoulder. The cheery clerk might be trying to cover up her despair over an abusive marriage, or she might be someone who loves her job and genuinely wants others to feel good. When we look at these very ordinary situations in terms of each individual's wants, it becomes a complex interweaving of desires and reactions—the perfect fodder for a story or poem.

4. *Look at the results.* What impact did this event have on you and on the other characters in your story? Did your encounter with the man in the supermarket make you feel defeated and depressed, or did you feel a welling up of compassion for him when you saw how troubled he seemed? How did it affect the man himself? Did the clerk's smile heal you from the dreadful day you were having, or did it simply annoy you that someone could be so cheerful? Again, we're not trying to read other people's minds. We are growing a story from our imaginations: reality is only the seed.

5. *Write.* By now, you have all the ingredients. Sit down and write them in whatever form suits you—a personal essay, a short story, a poem. Don't try to devise a perfect plot or the snappiest dialogue. Just let the story flow from your fingers onto the page. Allow it to grow and change shape as you write. Perhaps the shopping-cart guy changes from a blustering, beefy man to a neatly coifed woman in high heels. Maybe you find yourself morphing into someone brassier, sneakier, or wittier than you really are as the story develops. The events might even change as you go. There is no need to stick with a specific script. Let your imagination go.

———————————————{ SACRED TOOL }———————————————

Discovering Story Seeds in the World around You

Stories are like cottonwood trees in the spring: their seeds are everywhere, floating all around us, sticking on whatever they can cling to. You can find the kernel of a story in a casual conversation, the news, your dreams, a political speech. They appear in advice columns and radio call-in shows, religious sermons and scientific reports, jokes and geography textbooks. All you need is a sound technique for discovering them:

1. *Set your intention.* Start your day with the promise that before you go to bed that night, you are going to find a set number of story seeds—five or ten or even twenty, if you like pushing the envelope.

2. *Collect the seeds.* Keep a notebook with you and jot down whenever a story seed appears. Note that you aren't searching for a set number of *stories* or even ideas for stories. Having a good story idea implies a fairly clear notion of the characters and plot, such as, "After a

near-death experience, a woman develops the ability to see into the future" or "Two children discover a dead body and never tell their parents." A story seed is simpler and more basic. Here is a list of story seeds one writer found in a single day:

→ You think you've won a contest but find out you didn't.

→ You slip on the ice, and wrapped Christmas presents fall in the mud.

→ You are sitting in a boring meeting trying really hard to keep awake.

→ You want to watch a TV show, but your kids keep interrupting and you miss the best part.

→ You hear that a friend was hurt in an accident and you're really worried; then you find out that her injuries were mild.

3. *Grow the seeds into ideas for stories.* As they stand, none of the seeds listed above are ideas for stories, but each of them is a kernel from which a story might grow. At the end of the day, go over your list and come up with three ideas for stories. Here is one of the ideas that came out of the list of story seeds above:

> *A man is desperately trying to keep awake in a boring meeting*
> *at work. He tries to focus but finally falls asleep and dreams that*
> *he is running out of his office ripping his clothes off. Someone*
> *asks him a question, and he wakes up with a start, blurting out,*
> *"I'm free!" He is humiliated in front of his coworkers—but he*
> *also realizes he is miserable in his job and decides to quit.*

Of course, a story about someone falling asleep in a meeting could be developed in hundreds—perhaps thousands—of different ways. Maybe the sleepy person is a woman who was up late with a crying baby. Perhaps he is someone who suffers from debilitating insomnia. Maybe a coworker comes up later and asks if she is all right—the beginning of a love affair or friendship. The point is that every story seed contains the potential for an infinite number of stories. Be creative. The possibilities are endless.

CARING FOR STORIES

"If stories come to you, care for them," says Badger in Barry Lopez's *Crow and Weasel*.[5] Stories, like living beings, need to be nurtured. It isn't enough to merely receive them. For them to flower, they must be sheltered, nourished, and allowed to rest and grow.

The way to do this will differ depending on the story and your relationship to it. Some stories are full of energy. They rush at you, begging to be told, and hurry to find their way to the page. Many others are timid. You know they're lurking behind the hedge—they peek at you from time to time—but when you turn to see them, they duck down again. Others sit like big, lumpy ogres staring at you across the table. You are positive there's something good underneath all that fat, but it's going to take work to turn it into something lean and focused.

All of these types of stories need to be held, caressed, and nourished. How you nourish your story will depend on what that story needs.

—————————————————{ SACRED TOOL }—————————————————

Giving Your Story Time

When you have the seed of a story—or the first page, or a hastily scribbled draft—allow it to breathe for a time before attempting to refine it. How long you wait depends on the story and on your personal writing process. Some writers actually hold stories for months or even years before committing them to the page—but a few days is more common. Try these techniques for allowing stories to rest:

1. *Think of your story as an infant.* Although it possesses all that it will eventually need to become whole, at this point, it can't speak or act on its own. Imagine having to care for your story as you would a newborn. Sometimes you leave it alone to sleep, but you also spend a lot of time trying to keep it happy.

2. *Carry your story with you.* Symbolically infuse a stone or other small object with your story, then carry it in your pocket or purse. From time to time, you might pull it out to hold and watch—or you might forget about it until you discover it again, under the drugstore receipt at the bottom of your handbag.

3. *Set mindfulness intervals.* At some Buddhist monasteries, a bell is chimed at random intervals throughout the day. It is a reminder to the monks to be mindful of what they are doing at that minute. You can use a similar technique for a story. Set clocks or timers to go off when you won't be expecting it. Whenever you hear that chime, bring your mind back to your story. Perhaps you will simply think, "Oh, yeah. I'm still carrying that story around." But you may find that it has grown, changed shape, developed.

4. *Engage the sleep state.* Before you fall asleep at night, think of your story briefly. This reminder may help the story grow in your subconscious as you sleep. When you first open your eyes in the morning, allow the story to emerge. See if it has changed.

These practices allow our stories time to take root. They let them rest while not allowing them to drop completely out of awareness. Sometimes this simple gift of time is all a story needs to reach its full potential. Other times, a story may need more.

——————————————————————{ SACRED TOOL }——————————————————————

Nourishing Stories

Seeds need water and nutrients; infants need their mother's milk. Your story may need to be nourished as well. Once it has rested, you may feel it is still not ripe. Try these ways of feeding your story:

1. *Write character bios.* Explore your characters by writing their biographies. Whether you are working on a memoir or pure fiction, you can explore the people who populate your stories by writing lives for them. In this exercise, you get to know your characters beyond the limits of the story. Even if your work will say nothing about a character's relationship with his father, develop that relationship, and include it in his bio. Even if your story will not show your character getting up in the morning, write a description of her morning routine. You can't cover every aspect of your characters' lives, of course, but pick some part and go into detail. Don't just focus on the major events: consider the little things that annoy your characters, what they do on Sunday afternoon, what they eat for breakfast.

2. *Use the "what if" approach.* This technique helps you explore the latent richness of your story. Once you have a draft of your story down, go through it scene by scene with an awareness of the countless possibilities they present. For each scene or turn of events, ask yourself what could happen that would change the course of the story. What if the character forgot his wallet, fell on the stairs, or ran out in front of a bus? Perhaps the lovers are interrupted by a drunk neighbor.

The Sacred Gift 19

Maybe the children arguing in the playground witness a car crash. Brainstorm possibilities. Be as far-fetched or as realistic as you wish, but don't get carried away in the number of ideas you come up with. Once you start thinking about the countless things that could happen, it's easy to get overwhelmed.

Once you have several ideas, pick one that speaks to you in some way—or just randomly select one. Then write from that new angle. See what comes up as you write, where the fresh twist in the action takes you, and how it affects your characters. Many times, you will find that this helps you sharpen and focus the original premise of the story—and it can give you new insights into the characters. Sometimes you will find yourself with a whole new story that is richer than the one you started with.

3. *Write outside the scene.* All writers learn quickly that they will write many passages that eventually get sent to the "recycle bin," but some are surprised to learn that they can gain something from deliberately writing scenes they aren't going to use in their final piece. When we write outside the scene, we are not exploring new twists and turns in the plot, but rather adding to what is already there. Read your story and find a scene that seems particularly vivid or crucial—or just one you like. Now write what happens immediately before the scene starts and immediately after the scene is over. What were the characters doing before they met in the shoe store? What happened after they left? Simply show what the characters are doing, how they are feeling, and what they are thinking about when they aren't in the story. If their thoughts and behavior are prosaic or commonplace, don't worry. You are not writing material to incorporate into the story: you are delving into the characters, striving to get deeper insights.

Stories and Personal Transformation

Among indigenous peoples the world over, stories serve to reinforce ethical behavior, maintain social mores, and impart values. Many cultures hold storytelling in high esteem because they know that stories can effect personal and social change. In the West, we tend to think of stories as mere entertainment, forgetting that they also serve to guide, enlighten, and transform us. There are a number of ways we can employ stories as prompts to insight and growth.

────────────{ SACRED TOOL }────────────

Creating a Story Mandala

Many Buddhist and Hindu sects use *mandalas*—geometric depictions of the cosmos—to make the vastness of the Universe graspable and to focus the "monkey mind"—the chaotic, rapidly changing state of mind most of us experience most of the time. Mandalas have many uses—meditation, self-exploration, psychotherapy—and take a wide variety of forms, depending on their purposes and the spiritual traditions to which they belong.

Stories and mandalas have much in common. They both represent the Universe in microcosm and present a way to organize the confusion of human existence. As objects of meditation and vehicles for self-exploration, stories, like mandalas, offer us ways to find focus and discover meaning in the apparently random workings of the world.

Making a mandala from your story can give you fresh, often remarkable, insights. It can help you see the relationships between characters, scenes, and ideas. A story mandala can also allow you to identify places where the story falters—especially places that are over- or underwritten or that simply don't belong. By taking your linear, language-based work and translating it into a visual, spatial medium, you are called on to use different mental faculties and parts of the brain. Often, the result is a surprising new awareness. Creating a story mandala entails a few simple steps:

1. *Familiarize yourself with mandalas.* If you are unfamiliar with mandalas or need some ideas to get started, many Internet sites and a number of good books are available. You will find all sorts of different designs from various cultures and eras. Pay special attention to any that you find particularly beautiful or intriguing.

2. *Choose your material.* There are many ways to make a mandala: it may be painted or drawn, created on a computer, or constructed out of stones, sand, or textiles. Probably the easiest and, for our purposes, most convenient way to make a mandala is to use paper and paint or colored pencil.

3. *Create the shape of your mandala.* The most basic way to begin a story mandala is to create a fairly large square in your chosen medium and add a circle, centering it within the square. Then divide your geometric shapes with lines that radiate out from the center or by overlaying a grid.

4. *Add your characters.* Once you have this simple foundation in place, create representations of your characters within the mandala. You may use a symbol for each character, or different colored shapes, the characters' names, or whatever else you wish. Place each character within or around the outside of your circle. The placement of your characters will vary according to their roles in the story. The central character will probably be in the center, with other characters at varying distances from the center. Some characters may be placed outside the square at the edges of your page. Characters who act

together or appear in the same scenes might be close to each other on the mandala.

5. *Indicate connections.* Continue developing your mandala by connecting the characters based on their relationships and the events of the story. A simple line, a bundle of lines, or a more elaborate chain or braid can run from one character to the next. In some places, the connections will intersect, loop together, or even become inextricably tangled.

6. *Embellish your mandala.* When your characters are placed in the mandala and the connecting elements of your story are represented, add whatever design elements, flourishes, or decoration you wish. You may fill in different areas with color, add additional designs, or do whatever feels right for this particular story. Your mandala may be highly intricate, brilliantly colored, and elaborately embellished or very simple and rendered in black and white. Take your time, use your intuition, and go with whatever seems suitable.

7. *Meditate.* When you have finished your mandala, meditate on it. Sit comfortably with the mandala in front of you and simply look at it. Don't judge it (or the story it is based on) and don't work at understanding it. Just look at it with an open mind, letting your thoughts come and go. If your mind goes off track and you find yourself worrying about tonight's dinner or the parking ticket you need to pay, gently bring it back to your story mandala. Don't chide yourself for getting off course—even veteran meditators don't stay perfectly focused for long.

You might try meditating on your story mandala a little every day for several days or you might want to do a longer, more intensive meditation. Doing it right before you go to bed and again briefly first thing in the morning works well for many writers. Experiment to discover what technique works best for you and see where it leads you.

This exercise can be used for a number of purposes. For one thing, it can provide insight into the structure of the story, even showing you where something is missing or excessive. It can help you understand the relationships between the characters and the events of the story. It can give you ideas for improving the story. Or it can allow you simply to rest with the story for a while and observe it without judgment.

Using Stories as Catalysts for Growth

After reading a scholar's analysis of one of his short stories, author Omar S. Castañeda said in considerable surprise, "So *that's* what that story was trying to tell me!"[6] The paradox of personal change through storytelling is that it often takes place when you are not expecting it. As we are writing away, our subconscious minds are often busy explaining, clarifying, and solving problems. Sometimes we have to go back and reread our own stories to unearth the possibilities they bring to light.

It is never a good idea to try to write morals into your stories—a didactic story doesn't enlighten readers; it just annoys them. Instead, let your intuition go to work as you write. When you have finished a work and have left it for a time, come back and read it with fresh eyes. There are a number of techniques you can use when you revisit a story:

1. *Examine your characters.* One important difference among story characters is the extent to which they change during the course of the story. Some characters are highly dynamic: they experience great epiphanies that fundamentally alter the way they live. Others are

static, apparently determined not to change regardless of what they have undergone. Many fall somewhere in between.

One way to use a story as a vehicle for growth is to explore the growth your characters have experienced—or refused to experience. Take each character individually—the central ones as well as those who are more marginal. Identify whether the characters have changed over the course of the story. You may have dynamic characters who are transformed by the end of the story, static characters who stay the same, or a combination of both.

Identify how the dynamic characters have changed. Remember that change can be good, bad, or simply neutral: your character may be neither better nor worse off at the end of the story, just different. Perhaps the character has turned his life around in some major way—or maybe he has just gained a tiny amount of insight. The character may behave differently at the end of the story than at the beginning, but remember that the change may simply be a realization, a decision, or a new feeling, attitude, or belief.

2. *Look for causes.* Ask yourself what brought about the change in these characters. What event or combination of events sparked their transformation? What forces acted upon them? For characters who remained static throughout the story, examine the reasons they did not change. Was it because they didn't experience the same things as the dynamic characters—or was it that they did experience the same things but reacted to them differently? Was there something in their life circumstances, their pasts, or their personalities that prevented them from changing?

3. *Apply the story to your life.* Now consider how the story applies to your own life. Are your challenges similar to those of your characters? Are you faced with decisions or dilemmas that resemble theirs? Perhaps

your story is about something you've already gone through: in this case, it may simply support the changes you've made in your own life. Stories, including the ones we write ourselves, offer us advice, suggest alternatives, give us insights, show us possible results of our actions, and make us think about situations and conditions in new ways.

—————————————{ SACRED TOOL }—————————————

Creating a Story "Board Game"

This exercise offers another way to use stories as agents for personal transformation, taking a visual and spatial approach. You won't actually devise a board game in this exercise, but what you come up with may look like one. Each character will have a starting place on the board; most will have their own paths leading out of that starting place. The characters' experiences in the story move them along on their paths. A board game is easy to make:

1. *Create your board.* Use a fairly large blank piece of paper, such as that available in arts and crafts supply stores. Find an object to represent each character—a bead, pebble, or coin will work. As the story progresses, you will draw in the path each character takes and move the character along that path.

2. *Create a starting space for each character.* Use drawings or verbal descriptions to make the space represent the way your character feels and acts when she is first introduced.

3. *Indicate the character's movement.* When a character acts, or when something happens to her, she moves out of that space, and her path through the story begins. Each time she acts or experiences something, the path grows longer. When something changes her

awareness, feelings, attitude, or situation, her path changes direction. When characters interact, their paths on the board intersect. At any juncture where you feel it is important to identify the characteristics of the "place" or the state your character is in, do so in pictures or words.

When you have finished, most characters will be in a different spot from where they began—some will be quite far from their start spaces, others, closer. You may find that some characters barely stepped out of their start spaces—or came out for a time before making a U-turn and heading back in. In other words, you will have a spatial representation of the ways the characters have changed (or stayed the same) and the junctures in their lives that created those changes.

4. *Observe your "board game."* When you've completed tracking your characters' movements, leave your game for a while. Then come back to simply observe it. As you do, refrain from trying to "figure it out." Don't evaluate it, your story, or the characters. Simply accept the story and the representation you made of it for what they are. You might try coming back to it every couple of days for a few minutes or doing an extended writing meditation on it.

Remember that the goal of this exercise isn't a logical analysis. What we want is for the intuitive parts of our brains to go to work, using the visual representation we have given them. In this visible form, the story will act on us subtly and imperceptibly. We will come to know at some basic level how change takes place—in the lives of our characters as well in our own lives. At some point, we may say, like Castañeda, "So *that's* it!"

Offering Your Story

Among the Diné people—known to many as the Navajo—to be told a story is a great honor. In ancient Celtic cultures, storytelling was considered a service to the community. But contemporary writers seldom think of their work as a gift or service. Much has been written about how people heal themselves through writing—but almost nothing has been said about the ways writers can help heal another person, a community, or the Earth.

Envisioning your story as your personal gift is an acknowledgment of the significance and beauty of the work you are doing. It reminds you that you are not simply entertaining yourself or trying to find money or fame, but that your work has meaning and substance. It is vital that we keep this awareness alive. One way we can do this is to consciously alter our way of thinking of our stories so that we become aware that they are our gifts to the world:

1. *Begin by offering your story*. Before you begin to write each day, make a statement about the gift you are bestowing. Say aloud, "I offer my writing to the people of South America" or "This story is my gift to my grandmother and grandfather" or "This is for you, world." If you want to make the offering more concrete, write the statement down and place it somewhere you will see it regularly.

2. *Keep your gift in mind as you write*. It is easy to lose sight of the fact that our stories are offerings, especially as we become lost in our work—and all the egoistic feelings it brings up. Try to stop from time to time, as you write, and remind yourself. Look at the statement you wrote at the beginning. Read it aloud. Visualize yourself giving your story to others. Try to instill a deep feeling of generosity inside you as you work.

3. *Conclude by offering your story.* When you have finished a story, symbolically offer it. Light a candle and hold the story up toward the sky or close to your heart. Infuse it with your love. If you have a home altar, you can place it there for a time. Set it outside or by a window, in moonlight. Whatever you can do to ritualize your offering will confirm that you are bestowing a gift that is not only priceless, but unique in all the world.

———•◦•———

The purpose of all of these exercises is to help us see our stories in a new light. As you do them, you may find your relationship to your stories changing. Instead of considering them mere channels for your imagination, you may come to cherish them as the precious treasures that they are. Reminding ourselves of the true nature of stories—that they are vital and living things, sacred mandalas, vehicles for transformation, and our invaluable gifts to the world—reminds us that we are not engaged in mere record keeping or entertainment, but that we are doing sacred work.

Understanding that the supposedly ordinary act of storytelling is a work of great complexity and significance is the first step on the sacred path of writing. When you see stories as divine gifts, you can learn to be open to them, to wait for them with patience, and to recognize them when they come. Knowing their sacredness, you cannot do other than care for them. Being open to their wisdom allows you to use them as tools for personal transformation. Awareness that they are not ours to keep helps us pass them to others, not just as the work of our own creativity, but as a service to the world.

When we can truly honor stories as gifts, we are ready to delve more deeply into the sacred nature of writing. In the next part, we will look at the ways writing can lead us from our everyday experience into a new awareness and a fresh perspective on reality—and even put us in touch with the great mysteries of the Universe.

PART I | *The Mystic*
Journey

It's hard to imagine that an Indian holy man, a second-century Christian hermit, and a follower of a modern Caribbean religious movement would have similar spiritual experiences. But for centuries, saints, prophets, and ordinary people from these and many other traditions have shared nearly identical experiences in which the qualities of everyday life are transformed, the boundaries of the self seem to fall away, and a kind of transcendent understanding arises.

These mystic states engage a heightened awareness of the Universe. They bring about the realization that all things present, past, and future are one, and inspire a feeling that the self is dissolving, merging with that great oneness. The mystic has the sense that she is operating in a realm outside of time and space and that she is in touch with a power outside of herself. Most fundamentally, the mystic state is an immediate, intuitive awareness of the Universe, the All, the Divine.

Depictions of the mystic experience tend to get tangled in contradiction. It is often said to involve a deep, inward journey, but it also entails a turning of the mind outward, an opening up to the universe. It is sometimes thought of as requiring great discipline, such as that practiced by yogis and Zen monks, and yet it allows a letting go, a freeing of the mind from everyday constraints. It has been compared to sleep, even to death,but has also been called a supreme awakening. In truth, the mystic state is so difficult to pin down because it is radically different from the way we normally experience the world.

As India's Kena Upanishad states, "Different It is from all that are known, and It is beyond the unknown as well."[1]

Few writers would call themselves mystics, but many admit to experiencing something like mystical or quasi-mystical states. Alfred Tennyson, William Blake, William Wordsworth, Walt Whitman, and Charlotte and Emily Brontë were all reputed to have had mystic experiences. Contemporary poet Gary Snyder laces his work with references to mystical or quasi-mystical experiences as does novelist Louise Erdrich. Percy Bysshe Shelley wrote of an "invisible influence, like an inconstant wind" that awakens the mind when a writer is at work—an influence we can neither predict nor control.[2] In a letter to his friend Trevor Hughes, Dylan Thomas gave an almost-perfect description of the sense of unity experienced by the mystic: "It is my aim as an artist," he wrote, "to prove beyond doubt to myself that the flesh that covers me is the flesh that covers the sun, that the blood in my lungs is the blood that goes up and down in a tree."[3]

Even writers whose feet remain firmly in the here and now can benefit from exploring the mystical elements of the writing life. Understanding the connections between mysticism and writing can help heighten our awareness and allow us to relinquish control, letting creative energies in. The exercises in this section may not lead you to union with the Source of All (or perhaps they might), but they will help engage a vital, free-flowing creativity.

{3}

Transcendent Awareness

IF YOU THINK THAT you've never come close to a mystic state, consider these experiences:

→ You look up from the notebook you have been writing in and are amazed to see that it is dark outside. You've been writing for hours, unaware that your foot is going to sleep and you were supposed to finish those reports on the consumer response to a new style garage opener.

→ As you write, words start coming to you from out of nowhere. They come so naturally that you feel as if they are streaming from a source outside of you.

→ You start a story about a man who has just lost his job, and soon you find that he's leaving his wife, buying a bus ticket, plotting a murder, all without consulting you first. He seems to be taking over the story, making his own decisions. The entire story seems to be a living thing, creating itself out of nothing.

If you've had any experiences like these, then you've entered a state called *flow*. In this quasi-mystical condition, your focus on your writing becomes so sharp that the rest of the world seems to melt away. A steady current of words and images comes to you. You feel energized, open, inspired. Your awareness shifts: you become conscious of things that are normally inaccessible and you are unaware of what is going on around you. You may feel like you are operating outside of time and space, that they have become irrelevant.[1]

Flow is not precisely the same as a true mystical state, but the two experiences are clearly linked. Both are *altered states of consciousness*—conditions that are neither sleep nor wakefulness, but something different from either. Both are nonrational experiences. In flow, as in the mystic state, time and space seem to have no meaning. Like the mystic, the writer in flow experiences a unique awareness of the Universe in which he seems to be in touch with something greater than himself.

No practice in the world can guarantee either mystical experiences or flow—both come unexpectedly, at unusual times, and often to unlikely people—but there are things writers can do to make themselves open to flow.

OPENING THE DOOR TO HEIGHTENED AWARENESS

It is no wonder that heightened awareness is part of the writer's experience—her work is to cast fresh light upon the world, to present ordinary life in extraordinary ways. To do that, all writers must cultivate the ability to see beyond the surfaces of the day-to-day world to the miraculous essence at its core. This heightened awareness comes of its own accord. It can never be forced—but it can be invited in.

Turning On Your Spotlight

In her book *Bird by Bird*, Anne Lamott writes about the "one-inch picture frame."[2] Some writers talk about "slicing the pie" or "a single snapshot." They are all referring to focus: homing in on one paragraph or scene or description and letting the rest be, for the time being. You do not have to think up the entire plot of your novel right now. You do not have to capture the essence of your childhood. You do not have to figure out how people in your future civilization on Pluto cultivate food. That can come later. All you have to work on at this moment is a narrow wedge of pie. You need to turn your spotlight on, bringing a small area into sharp focus, and let the rest retreat into shadow.

Turning off the "big picture" and concentrating your attention on a limited, clearly defined area is an excellent way to open yourself to flow. It clears your mind of confusion, uncertainty, and murkiness and allows all your energies to converge upon a single point. Into that clean channel rush the forces of creativity aiming straight for the heart of your work. There are several steps you can take to help you create a spotlight:

1. *Create a statement.* Write a single sentence that describes what you are going to work on right now. "Today, I will write about the white horse I saw running in the field near the water tower" or "This single snapshot is a picture of my cousin in her blue business suit" or "I am going to write about my father's woodworking tools." Don't just think the sentence: write it out. Then put it where you can see it while you write.

2. *Fill one sheet.* Another technique is to get out one piece of paper and tell yourself, "This is all I am going to fill right now." Concentrate on filling just that one sheet. Once it is full, you can decide whether to start a second. If you do, again concentrate only on filling that single

sheet. If you don't start a second sheet, you have still accomplished something significant: you've completed one full page of writing.

3. *Set a time limit.* Decide for yourself that all you have to do right now is write for one hour, or twenty minutes, or five minutes—whatever interval feels right. If you start feeling overwhelmed, remind yourself, "I'm not solving all my plot problems this moment: I'm just writing what I can in the next ten minutes."

Tomorrow, perhaps, you can take the time to consider the relationship between this paragraph and the next one, this character and all the others, this scene and the entire plot. But right now, focus on that thin slice and watch the ways it activates flow.

———————————————{ SACRED TOOL }———————————————

Point-of-Light Meditation

Flow comes when our minds are so focused on our writing that we become unaware of other sensory input. It is easy to see why this focus can be so difficult to attain at this time in the twenty-first century. Our senses are bombarded all day, every day, and our minds are always actively planning, figuring, observing, conversing, reading, and solving problems. We do not live in a reflective age: we have little practice in focusing our thoughts on one thing, and it is almost impossible for us to turn our brains off. So flow—like the mystic state—is hard to come by.

This point-of-light meditation uses imagery to evoke a sense of increased awareness while quieting the mind and screening out extraneous information:

1. *Prepare.* Find a place where you won't be disturbed, where it is relatively quiet and there are few distractions. Put your writing materials

where they will be ready and at hand. Sit comfortably with your body balanced and your spine straight. Find a posture that works for you, whether in a chair or on the floor. You should be comfortable and relaxed but be sitting in a position that allows you to remain alert.

2. *Focus*. Begin by breathing deeply in and out for several slow breaths. Focus your mind on the breath gently flowing in and out. Be aware of the movement in your body when you breathe and how the air feels in your nose and chest. If your mind goes off on a tangent, simply bring it gently back to the breath—without any irritation or straining.

3. *Visualize emptiness*. When your mind feels somewhat still, visualize a vast, empty darkness in front of you. Rest for a while in the stillness and silence, the no-mind of this void. Experience the emptiness.

4. *See the light*. Visualize a pinpoint of intense white light far in the distance, very small, but very bright. Try not to analyze what it is or what is happening. Just see it and remain focused on it.

5. *Ask the light to approach*. As you focus on the pinpoint of light, see it slowly become brighter and bigger. Imagine that it is approaching you. After a while, the pinpoint becomes a small disk, then a larger one as it steadily moves toward you. Very gradually, the light takes up more and more of your field of vision. As the light becomes larger, the darkness shrinks. After a time, it is the light that dominates, with the darkness narrowing in the periphery.

6. *Continue watching the light*. Keep observing the light without expectations and without attempting to analyze it. If you lose focus, don't get frustrated, just return your thoughts gently to the light and continue to watch it get larger and larger. Eventually, the light fills up the dark space. You see everything—the entire cosmos—in the brilliant light. You are bathed in that light.

7. *Write*. Maintain your state of openness and vision as you let your words emerge. Remember that your goal is not to produce the perfect poem right now, but to allow the process of flow to operate in you. If you find yourself starting to control your writing—to question, self-edit, or hesitate—rest for a moment, breathe deeply, and visualize that astonishing light. Continue writing with that brilliant light all around you.

LETTING IDENTITY FADE

St. Teresa of Avila described her mystic experiences as a "self-forgetfulness" so overpowering that she felt her soul had ceased to exist.[3] This loss of identity— a sense that the boundaries of your self have dissolved and you are disappearing as a separate entity—is common to mystic states. As the mystic realizes the Oneness of everything, his ego seems to merge with that great All.

Writers also experience a loss of self, albeit a less dramatic one. When you are fully engaged in your writing, the ego seems to disappear—if only for a moment—and your own identity falls away. You cease to live your own life for a time and you inhabit the world you are creating. Although this often happens spontaneously, you can open yourself to the experience by relaxing your grip and allowing a softening of the boundaries of the self.

—————————{ SACRED TOOL }—————————

Floating Away

This exercise uses the "corpse position" familiar to practitioners of yoga. Don't let the name put you off—it's an unpleasant moniker for a pleasant experience. From this position, the exercise leads you on a sublime journey:

1. *Lie in perfect relaxation.* With your writing materials ready to take up, begin this exercise by lying on your back on a mat or rug on the floor—beds are generally too soft. Your hands should be resting by your side, and your legs should be straight and slightly apart. Many people find it most relaxing to lie with their palms facing up. For a few moments, simply be present on that spot. Drop your awareness down to your body, letting other concerns fade away. Be conscious of the physical part of you: the blood and bones, the muscles and organs. Feel the weight of your body as it is pulled down by gravity. Feel its mass as it occupies space.

2. *See your body as a vessel.* When you have become fully aware of your body, picture it as a vessel that contains who you are. Your body still has mass, it still takes up space and presses against the ground, but you are now aware that it isn't you—it is merely a shell you occupy. Rest with that awareness.

3. *Feel the vessel growing lighter.* Imagine your body growing slightly lighter, losing substance and weight. Gradually feel it becoming lighter still and less substantial, and as it lightens, see it becoming less solid. Very slowly, let your body lose its mass. See the muscle and bone fade, until they are transparent and ghostlike.

4. *Allow your body to float in air.* Lie for a moment in this ethereal state, absorbing the sense of lightness and transparency. Then feel your body lift slowly off the rug as if it is floating upward. See it hover a few inches above the rug, then, as it becomes lighter still, see it float upward.

5. *Become a breath.* By now, your body is as light and insubstantial as a bubble. Little more than a shadow, it easily floats through the roof of your house and continues to float upward into the atmosphere, farther and farther away. The Earth becomes small as this ethereal self

continues to move gently into the vastness of the Universe. Finally, the bubble bursts. You are now nothing but a breath. Allow yourself to feel for a while what it is to be only a breath.

6. *Write*. Sit up slowly. Breathe deeply, remain relaxed, and write. As well as you can, keep that feeling of being nothing more than a breath as you write. See what comes out of that selfless state. When you feel yourself sinking back to Earth and becoming solid, pause for a moment. Close your eyes and remember that feeling of lightness and transparency. Float away again and become a breath. Continue writing.

This exercise is intended to be a pleasant experience, and most find it to be. However, a few writers react to it with anxiety. If it seems frightening to envision your body disappearing this way, avoid doing this exercise. This isn't a case where you should challenge yourself to confront your fear: there are many exercises in this book that do that. Instead of forcing yourself through this meditation, do the point-of-light meditation.

GIVING OVER CONTROL

When poet Tess Gallagher begins to write, she has the feeling that her poetry is already written—it is just waiting for her to get it down on paper.[4] Novelist Christina Adam sees stories in front of her as a kind of dream.[5] Virtually all writers have the feeling at least some of the time that their stories are coming from something other than themselves, just as mystics sense the presence of a power or consciousness other than their own. Certain exercises can set the stage for this sense.

Allowing the Stones to Speak

Virtually all stories are written from the viewpoints of people—or animals imbued with humanlike consciousness. This exercise encourages us to think from odd, unexpected points of view, to shift our imaginations in ways that can force us to relax our control:

1. *Absorb the sense of a story or poem.* Pick a story or poem you've written. If you wish, you can also do this exercise with the work of another author. Begin by reading the work over once or twice. When you feel as if you've gotten a strong intuitive sense of the story, set it down.

2. *Write as an inanimate object.* Consider the viewpoint of an inanimate object in the story—a necklace one of the characters is wearing, a coffee cup someone uses, a mirror, a stone in someone's yard. Spend a few moments imagining the consciousness of the object. Think of what it would experience if it had awareness—consider what it would be like to be that coffee mug or the rearview mirror in a character's car. Rewrite the story from the object's point of view. As you write, give yourself over to the thoughts of the object. Allow it to "speak." What do these entities have to say about what is happening around them? Do their own "experiences" and basic nature alter their perception in strange and unexpected ways? Pay attention to the nature of the object as you imagine it to be and incorporate it into the object's voice. Does the rock have a particularly rigid, impenetrable viewpoint or one that has become hardened through the eons it has "lived"? Does the river think quick, clear thoughts? Does the leaf open to the things around it as it does to the sun? What can an entity so different from ourselves add to our understanding?

3. *Let the story lead.* Sometimes this shift in point of view sends the story off into an entirely different direction—if so, let it go. Relinquish your former concept of the story. This doesn't mean you should throw your earlier ideas out—you may come back to them later—but for the time being, release them and follow the story. Allow it to lead you where it will.

—————————————————{ SACRED TOOL }—————————————————

The Voice of the Other

Another way to let go of control over your work is to allow your words to come from sources outside yourself. Do this exercise when you are beginning a new work or revising a previously written one. As with the "Allowing the Stones to Speak" exercise, this requires you to temporarily suspend your original vision. Once again, the key to this exercise is surrender:

1. *Stop and borrow.* At various intervals as you write, stop. This can be at the end of every paragraph, at the beginning of each new page, or at two-minute intervals, indicated by a timer. Borrow the next line of your work from a source outside of you and over which you have no control. The most common way to find the next line is by opening a book to a random page and blindly pointing to a line, but there are other possibilities. One author turns on the TV and uses the first sentence she hears. Writing groups sometimes work together. They spend five minutes writing, then each person supplies the next line for someone else's work—without even knowing what the work is about. If you do use the more common book method, be creative in the type of book you use. You are not restricted to works of literature: try comic strips, technical manuals, cookbooks, or your childhood diary.

2. *Follow the line*. After you find the line, begin your next sentence with it—then follow where that thought takes you. Don't just write the line and go back to the work you were already doing. Let the line take you to new territory, no matter how awkward, off-topic, or silly it seems. Remember that your purpose is to give up control of your writing—and that you are trying to venture into a new kind of awareness.

Becoming One with the Universe

When a reader becomes lost in a story or poem, it is because the writer has touched upon something universal. No matter that her work is about particular people at a specific time and place: it springs from an intuitive grasp of the universal life of which we are all a part. In order to write with this kind of global awareness, the writer must experience something akin to the mystic's consciousness of oneness. To attain this awareness, we must be open to the Universe, listen carefully to what it is telling us, and celebrate our connections with it every chance we get.

———————————————{ SACRED TOOL }———————————————

A Message from the Universe

The literary work that we do may seem unrelated to the movement of the planets or the evolution of life on Earth. In truth, it has everything to do with them. Our poems and stories grow from the same great creative forces of the cosmos. They are one manifestation of the creative spirit that pervades the Universe.

It is easy to forget this all-important connection, but keeping it in mind can infuse life into our writing. This exercises engages meditation to help you visualize that connection:

1. *Prepare.* Make sure you are in a quiet place where you won't be disturbed. Make yourself comfortable. Have your writing materials ready and nearby.

2. *Center yourself.* Breathe deeply and feel your body relaxing. Take as long as you need to create a state of deep calm and focus.

3. *Visualize this scene.* Keeping your relaxed state, engage all your senses to create this scene in your mind:

> *You are on a beach, alone. The sand is soft under your feet. The sun warms your face. The breeze from the ocean is salty and bracing. Glassy waves lap the shore gently. All you see is the endless sea and the beach stretching out into the distance. All you hear are the waves and the occasional distant call of a gull. You are strolling, barefoot, down the beach. You are serene and happy as you continue to walk.*
>
> *You see something in the sand ahead of you. As you walk toward it, you realize it is a shell, the kind you can put to your ear and hear the rush of air. You approach it, stoop, and pick it up.*
>
> *You hold the shell in your hand, feeling its weight and texture. Is it cool and smooth or has it been warmed by the sun? Does it feel heavy and dense or light and airy? Smell it and study its surface.*
>
> *Know this: The shell is very old. It has been waiting in the sea for a long time. It has been waiting for you. The sea has brought*

it up right at this time, for you to find. What it has to say is for
you alone. Put it to your ear. What does it tell you?

4. *Write.* When you are ready, begin writing. Imagine that you are listening to the shell, that it is giving you the words you are writing. Do not question what comes up. Be open and receptive to whatever the shell is saying. If you feel you are losing touch with the message, pause for a moment and listen. If the message stops, continue listening for a moment: the shell may have more to say. When it becomes completely silent, accept the fact that it has no more to say right now. Visualize yourself putting it back on the sand or giving it back to the sea, but know that you may visit it again. It may have much more to say.

-----------------------------{ SACRED TOOL }-----------------------------

Tracing the Life of an Atom

One of the surprises of modern science is the realization that the atoms that make up our bodies have existed since the Big Bang and will continue to exist until the end of the Universe. A hydrogen atom in a drop of your blood may many times have been a part of the ocean or a cloud—on this planet or another. It may have been in the cells of untold numbers of plants and animals. It has no doubt been in drinking water, urine, icebergs, pomegranates, comets, and earthworms. It has probably been part of thousands of human bodies before becoming part of yours. Perhaps it was in the tears of a prehistoric woman whose child had died or in the heart of an Amazonian hunter or in the doomed Hindenburg zeppelin. This exercise can remind us of this remarkable unity:

1. *Write the atom's history.* With these myriad possibilities in mind, write a history of one hydrogen atom that is in a drop of your own blood. What route did that single atom take through the eons? How did it get from one place to another? Did evaporation move it from the ocean to the sky? Did a little boy's peeing in the snow move it from his body to the ground? Be as specific and detailed as you can.

2. *Write the atom's future.* Now go in the other direction: when this atom leaves your body, where might it go and how? Imagine it traveling through the future. Visualize all the things it may one day be part of.

WHEN FLOW WON'T COME

If you don't experience flow when you write, don't despair. Not every writer goes into it easily—some very brilliant writers say they never have flow experiences.

But what if you strongly hope to experience the freedom and energy of flow and just can't seem to beckon it? One aspect of flow is that *trying* to go into it seldom works. In fact, the more effort you put out, the less likely you are to succeed. This means that the best thing you can do is to accept the creative place you are in right now. Acknowledge that space, and honor it for what it is. Paradoxically, that acceptance of the lack of flow is sometimes exactly what we need to open to the flow experience.

───────────────{ SACRED TOOL }───────────────

Practicing Acceptance

Most often, we try to handle blocks by beating them into submission or trying to pretend that they aren't there. It works much better to accept them when they come. One way to do this is to acknowledge that you can't write right now—and then write anyway. This double-edged exercise sounds peculiar, but it works:

1. *Acknowledge the blockage.* Say to yourself, "This just isn't a productive period for me. The ideas aren't coming, and my writing feels flat and stilted. Okay, then for the time being, I'm just going to live with that."

2. *Write anything.* Once you've acknowledged your block, don't use it as a reason to go swimming or head for the mall. Instead, pick up your pen, put it to the page, and write. Nothing's coming? Create a list of your favorite TV shows. Write a description of the freckles on your hand. Pen a letter to the editor of your local paper, voicing some grievance. Write about the things you need to do around the house or the errands you have to run. Write a paragraph about everything you wish were different about your life—and then write one about the things you love about your life. Write a recipe. Write a to-do list. Keep your pen to the page (or your fingers on the keyboard), even as you accept the fact that, for the time being, your writing is uninspired.

3. *Write from the here and now.* So you have no ideas. No ingenious plots are coming to you. No melodic phrases or stunning metaphors are appearing. You want your creative energies to soar, but they are remaining firmly on the ground. Just write what is on your mind right now. You might write, "I can't think of a damn thing to write, and all I want to do is go to the pier and stick my feet in the cool water and watch the ducks. I feel like I have ideas inside my head, but I just can't get them from there onto the page. Also, I really want a piece of pound cake" or "I'm so tired today and I'm upset because I bounced that check last week" or "I'm sitting at my desk and I have a zit on my forehead and I can hear the sprinkler running in the yard." Write what you see out your window this minute, what you read in the newspaper that morning, a joke from the late-night

talk-show monologue you heard last night, the fact that your left eye is itchy. One possibility is to simply list what you see around you at this moment, what sounds you are hearing, whatever bodily sensations you may be having. Don't worry about making it into a work of art—that's leaving the here and now for the there and then. Write from the right here and right now, and you might discover yourself entering the quasi-mystical state of flow when you least expect it.

———•·•———

For a very few writers, true mystic states may be natural and easily come by. But for many those states are extremely rare. For the great majority of us who will never know a full mystical experience, a state of flow can produce some of the heightened awareness, sense of connection, and release of boundaries that the mystic undergoes. Flow opens us up to surging creative forces, whether you see those as coming from within or from something outside of yourself. It can spark currents of surprising energy and inspiration.

The quasi-mystical experience of flow is one powerful way to charge our writing. But even if we never experience flow, there is still much we can learn from the mystic. This is because people who have had mystical experiences tend to experience life somewhat differently from others. They have perspectives that are all their own. In the next chapter, we will explore the off-kilter ways mystics see the world and experiment with techniques to develop our own uniquely skewed perspectives.

{4}

Crazy Wisdom

WHEN PHOTOGRAPHER Demetri Dimas Efthyvoulos was developing his pictures of the Amazon, he thought he had created nothing more than some beautiful photos. Then something told him to turn the pictures sideways so that the river ran vertically down the page, and a whole world of images emerged—including faces of what appear to be spirits, demons, and deities. This unique way of seeing—which Efthyvoulos calls *side sight*—captures the spirit of the crazy wisdom that lies at the heart of mystic vision.[1]

Crazy wisdom means abandoning preconceived notions, seeing through surfaces, and moving beyond ordinary reason. It is a wisdom built of multiple perspectives, irreverence, paradox, and a love of the absurd. Buddhist teacher and writer Wes Nisker calls it "the wisdom of the saint, the Zen master, the poet, the mad scientist, and the fool."[2] It is the stuff of myth, the things that make sense in dreams but become absurd upon waking. It is also the wisdom of the writer. It is what enables us to pay attention to the odd and out of balance, to embrace the strange and contradictory in our world, just as the mystic does.

SEEING SLANT

According to Emily Dickinson, the poet should "tell the truth but tell it slant."[3] In fact, the writer must be able to *see* things slant as well. A survey of the world's mystics shows that they are almost always people who perceive the world in ways that seem off-kilter to everyone else. A similarly skewed point of view can help the writer cultivate perception of the oddness, paradox, and absurdity in daily life.

{ SACRED TOOL }

Reverse Lateral Thinking

In 1967, a psychologist named Edward de Bono coined the phrase *lateral thinking* to describe a type of reasoning that involves altering your assumptions in unusual ways.[4] Here is a typical lateral-thinking, problem-solving exercise:

A child falls from the tenth story of a building. He has no parachute or similar device, and his fall is not broken by an awning, tree, or anything else. He lands on bare rocks—but he isn't hurt. How could that happen?

The first response of most people to this question is that, if the boy is a normal human, it is simply impossible. But by employing lateral thinking—coming up with answers that alter our normal experiences of the world—you might arrive at the conclusion that one side of the building is next to a cliff, the top of which is only a foot lower than the tenth story. Lateral-thinking puzzles may be fairly simple like this example, but there are many whose solutions require truly original ways of thinking. All of them force you to reject some common assumptions. That's a difficult feat because most of the time we aren't even aware we're making assumptions.

Doing lateral-thinking puzzles is, in itself, an excellent way to stimulate off-kilter thinking—some good lateral-thinking puzzle books are available, and there are many such puzzles on the Internet. But in this exercise we are going to use something we will call *reverse lateral thinking*. It is "reverse" only in that you start out not with a puzzle that someone has given you, but with a scenario you create yourself:

1. *Create a list of impossible scenarios.* The situations should appear to be something that simply couldn't happen. For example, you might come up with something like this:

   > In the middle of a terrible lover's quarrel, Mary told Jake to leave her apartment and never come back. Hanging his head, Jake left, and Mary locked the door. When she went into the kitchen, there he was.

   As you're coming up with your scenarios, don't do them with solutions in mind. Part of the challenge is to have to work to solve your own puzzles.

2. *Don't think too hard.* The more we think about these improbable scenarios, the harder they are to come up with. The logical parts of our brains don't want to create such paradoxes and balk at devising situations without obvious conclusions. It is easy to overthink them, trying to get at the "best" off-kilter scenario you can. It works better to come up with them as spontaneously as you can.

3. *Challenge the clock.* Set a timer for three minutes and create as many of these absurd situations as you can before the alarm goes off. They don't need to be any more elaborate than the one about Mary and Jake above, but try to vary them. An important component of this exercise is speed. Dash them out as fast as possible. This will challenge your imagination and will also keep you from being too analytical.

4. *Solve your own puzzles*. When the bell goes off, stop. Go back and read the situations you came up with—and solve them. To truly challenge yourself, try coming up with three solutions for each one. Don't engage fantasy when you solve the solutions. If you imagine that one of the characters suddenly sprouted wings or had the ability to become invisible, you aren't really solving the puzzle, just finding an ad hoc response. Instead, try to find an explanation that would work in the real world—that's a much greater challenge.

{ SACRED TOOL }

Forced Analogy

Creating and recognizing analogies is a fundamental writing skill—in fact, a fundamental part of being human. But crafting analogies from dissimilar things gives us a different kind of challenge, making us see unusual and unexpected connections. It would be trite to say, "Little girls' voices are like babbling brooks," but what if we said, "Little girl's voices are like palm trees"? Our first reaction to such an analogy might be that there is simply nothing we can do with it. It is only after looking at it with a somewhat skewed viewpoint that we can work with it. Can we say that the girls' voices and the palm trees are both thin and high, that they are both graceful, that the voices resemble the fluttering of a palm frond? Use your imagination. Coming up with these unusual comparisons requires nothing more than a willingness to experiment:

1. *Pick your terms*. Open a book to a random page and pick the first noun or verb you come to. Then repeat the process and pick a second noun or verb. On a sheet of paper, write a statement comparing the two. If the two words you picked randomly were "exercising" and "peaches," write "Exercising is like peaches. . . ."

2. *Find comparisons.* Below the heading, brainstorm ways you could compare the two. You might come up with something like:

> *Exercising is like peaches. . . .*
> *They are both good for you.*
> *They are both a little messy.*
> *The further you go into them, the damper they get.*

Come up with as many as you can.

Although you may from time to time devise a brilliant analogy doing this exercise, most of the ones you come up with will probably be strained and awkward like the ones above. The point of the exercise isn't necessarily to craft material to use in your poetry and fiction—although that may happen—but to expand your creativity and give yourself a chance to practice seeing things "slant."

────────────────{ SACRED TOOL }────────────────

Synaesthesia

We might describe a rose as "red," "plump," and "many petaled" and we might describe a musical note as "shrill," "booming," or "chiming." But what happens when we describe a musical note as "yellow" or a word as "oval," a day of the week as "rectangular," the taste of a candy bar as "wavy"? *Synaesthesia* refers to mixing or confusing different senses. Some people do it naturally—they automatically see different colors when they hear musical tones or envision days of the week as being certain shapes. But even if you aren't someone who perceives the key of D as blue and Thursday as a square, you can employ synaesthesia. In fact, we already do this without knowing it when we refer to a sound as "soft" or a taste as "sharp." By pushing ourselves a bit further and using more unusual forms of synaesthesia, we can begin to fashion our own unique perspectives and help ourselves break out of preconceived notions. You can use any combination of senses:

1. *Describe visual objects as sounds.* Pick a passage from something you have written or from the work of some writer you admire. Rewrite it, describing visual objects as sounds:

   + A raucous wall

   + A lilting coffee cup

   + The sun setting in the key of B flat

   + A chair with an Italian accent

2. *Paint smells and tastes with color:*

   + The purple aroma of boiled turnips

   + The scarlet taste of raw onion

3. *Give sounds form and texture:*

   + Her hard and square voice

   + His squishy piece on the untuned piano

4. *Play with the possibilities.* Come up with different combinations. Give an odor a sound or color. Give a sound a taste or smell. Give a normally silent object a voice or melody.

{ SACRED TOOL }

Writing from Oxymora

Oxymora—phrases that contradict each other, like "clean dirt" or "a merry sadness"—create paradoxes that can open us to crazy wisdom. In fact, the term *crazy wisdom* is almost an oxymoron itself. Oxymora are not difficult to come up with and they can offer a gateway to the eccentric creativity we are aiming for. This exercise starts with oxymora and runs with them:

1. *Come up with oxymora.* Set a timer for sixty seconds and write as many oxymora as you can come up with. Be as creative as you can, as long as your phrases consist of two terms that contradict. If you're like most people, an "easy physics class" is an oxymoron as are a "boring bungee jump" and a "pleasant colonoscopy."

2. *Select some oxymora to write with.* When you have written a substantial set of them, pick a few that stand out or seem especially apt and use them as prompts for five-minute writing meditations.

3. *Write an oxymoron poem.* You can also try writing a poem based on one of the oxymora, or a poem incorporating three or more of them.

{ SACRED TOOL }

Nonsense Words

Most of us are familiar with the most famous work built from nonsense words: Lewis Carroll's "Jabberwocky." The interesting thing about this poem is that we can easily find meaning in it, even though, in isolation, many of the words are meaningless. This is because even nonsense words hint at meanings by the way they are used and from the way they sound.

We can use nonsense words in our own writing to stimulate the creative use of vocabulary and to increase our awareness of the sounds of our language and how those sounds work. Nonsense words can be used in a couple ways:

1. *Write a nonsense-word poem.* Write a poem in which every third noun is a nonsense word. Instead of writing, "When I think of Susan in the park, I think of *rain* " write, "When I think of Susan in the park,

I think of brosfures." Make your nonsense words pronounceable, so that you can read it aloud when you are finished—in other words, use *vomes* and *feeb* rather than *xlmn* and *kbqd*. When you are finished, read your poem aloud. Then adjust the nonsense words, replacing any that don't work.

2. *Write about the poem.* When you've completed the poem, write about its meaning. You don't have to be too analytical; just explore what it might mean, and if you don't see any obvious meaning in it, just explore its tone and how it makes you feel.

3. *Share your poem.* It can be interesting to read your poem to someone, or have them read it, and ask them what they think it means. See if their intuitive response is similar to yours or radically different.

4. *Create nonsense definitions.* Make up ten nonsense words. Include some that sound like short, basic words (*buke, flom, jeeb*) and others that seem more like academic words (*exfraxate, dysmornial*). Now come up with definitions for your words. If you can, create definitions for things that have no names in any language you know. For example, one writer created the word *awalp* and said it was the way you feel after eating too many bananas. Another invented *griffity* for hair that is frizzy from humidity. You can also ask others what they think the words might be.

———————————————{ SACRED TOOL }———————————————

Engaging the Dream State

We are never closer to our own crazy wisdom than when we are dreaming. Dreams are not based on the rational processes of ordinary thinking, but on the intuitive and mythic modes of our unconscious minds. We don't have to try "seeing slant" in our dreams: paradox and absurdity are what they are made from.

Unfortunately, dreams are also elusive, slipping easily away when we open our eyes. Tapping into this remarkable resource can give us access to the strange and incongruous crazy wisdom that lies within. The best way to make use of this remarkable resource is to engage the transition state between sleep and wakefulness, when we are still in the hold of dream magic:

1. *Wake yourself in the night.* Have a notebook and pen ready next to your bed. Set an alarm to wake you up in the middle of the night— or whatever time you would usually be sound asleep. When it goes off, start writing immediately. Don't wait to stretch, yawn, look at the time, get out of bed, go to the bathroom, or anything else. If you were having a dream that you can remember when you wake up, you can write about it or use it as a starting point. If not, you can still use the disorientation of your half-asleep state as a doorway to crazy wisdom.

2. *Write first thing in the morning.* If you simply can't imagine waking yourself up in the middle of the night—or if your partner protests— try writing immediately upon waking in the morning. Again, don't wait until you are ready to write. It is the state of *unreadiness* that can open the door to unusual worlds. That morning cup of coffee or quick check of our email will promptly rouse us out of the dream state and into the ordinary logic of everyday life.

WORKING WITH THE BODY

We often forget how accustomed our bodies are to the routines in our lives— until we force them out of their habits. When we do more exercise than usual, get up at an unusual hour, don't eat a meal at the time we normally do, or eat food we aren't used to, our bodies react. A person who takes a specific route home every day will often find herself turning that way even when she plans to go someplace else. A two-year-old child who once burnt himself on a floor furnace in an old house grew up to be a man who never went near that furnace—even though he had no conscious memory of his injury. Our bodies have long memories—and they are surprisingly set in their ways.

For this reason, one of the most effective ways to move ourselves into the unexpected is to use our bodies in ways they aren't used to. This doesn't have to be anything dramatic. A few fairly simple exercises are enough to nudge us into a new mode.

{ SACRED TOOL }

Writing with the Other Hand

Because we are naturally right- or left-handed—and because we spend our entire lives using our dominant hand for most tasks—forcing ourselves to use the other, or nondominant, hand challenges our bodies to perform very familiar tasks in unfamiliar ways. Writing with the nondominant hand is believed to stimulate parts of the brain not normally used in writing. At the very least, it results in a sense of oddness, even disorientation, that can have some surprising effects on our writing. There are a number of ways writing with the "other" hand can be done:

1. *Rewrite earlier work.* Go to something you have already written— a poem, a paragraph, a scene—and rewrite it using your opposite hand. You may find yourself looking at the work with a fresh eye— and surprisingly different insights.

2. *Do a writing meditation.* Write for five minutes with your nondominant hand. Give yourself a five-minute break, then write for five

minutes on the same topic with the hand you usually use. When you are finished, compare the two pieces. Some people find that the two freewriting pieces are more or less the same; others are amazed at the differences. See what you find.

3. *Write haiku or other compact work.* Try writing haiku, very short stories, prose poems, or any other very concise form with your nondominant hand. This forces you to deal with two challenges at once: the use of your nondominant hand and the need to pack meaning into a highly structured format.

This exercise not only helps us generate the kind of fresh imaginative writing born of crazy wisdom, but it sometimes brings to our awareness writing habits and patterns we hadn't recognized before and gives us a chance to get rid of those patterns that are holding back our creativity.

Altering the Body

Another exercise that can force the body to deal with the unusual is to eliminate some part of it from your daily routine. *Be careful!* Losing such things as depth perception, peripheral vision, and the ability to localize sound can be dangerous when you haven't learned to deal with them appropriately. Don't drive or engage in any other activity that requires full attention and use of all your senses. It is important to take care when doing this exercise:

1. *Eliminate use of a body part.* Try going through a morning with one eye covered, with an ear plug in one ear, or without using one of your hands. (If you normally operate with one eye, ear, or hand, of course try not using a different body part.) Although most of us realize that using only one hand will require some adjustment, you may think

that removing the use of an eye or an ear won't—until you actually do it. With only one eye, you lose depth perception and much of your peripheral vision, and you may find after a time that you are looking at things differently. When you try to get by without the use of one ear, you will find that you don't hear as well, that even slight extraneous noise interferes greatly with your hearing (a car passing on the street outside can make the conversation you're engaged in completely unintelligible), and that you can't tell the direction sounds are coming from.

2. *Open up.* The objective of this exercise is *not* to show how difficult it is to have lost the use of a body part. Many people go through life just fine with one eye, ear, or hand—or with none. But they have had practice and have developed the skills to function well. Those who haven't had that experience must adjust swiftly to a new mode of operation, which opens up fresh perspectives.

3. *Write.* Some people like to take notes throughout the exercise. Others prefer to wait and write about it at the end. Either way, sit down when you have finished and write. Create a poem or story based on your experience, or freewrite about it. Or simply write a work *not* based on this exercise and see how the experience bleeds into your writing.

Altering Your Position to Alter Your Perspective

Writing in a physical position that is unusual for us—and not quite as cozy as our normal posture—can help spur us into a crazy wisdom state. Try these ways of altering your writing:

1. *Stand up.* If, like most writers, you work at a desk or table, try writing standing up.

2. *Try a different surface.* If you usually write in a recliner, try the desk for a change. If you're accustomed to a desk, try sitting on the floor. If you often write sitting on the floor, try a tall stool and your countertop.

3. *Explore other possibilities.* For most of us, those simple changes will feel strange and awkward enough. If you want to try something a little more extreme, try writing lying down, sitting in the lotus position, or in some other position that you normally don't write in.

PAYING ATTENTION

A well-known Zen story tells of a famous teacher who asked his student if he'd been practicing awareness every minute. "Yes!" the student answered enthusiastically. But when the teacher asked him if he'd placed his umbrella on the left or right side of his shoes when he entered the meditation hall, the student couldn't answer.

Unless we have done mindfulness practice for many years, we will find it impossible to pay moment-by-moment attention to the details of everyday life. Yet striving for that kind of careful attentiveness can lead us into new modes of thinking—and is an invaluable tool for the writer.

——————————————————{ SACRED TOOL }——————————————————

Focused Observation

Just like the Zen student in the story, we often go through our days without noticing the things around us. How many times have we seen and handled pennies? Yet can you accurately remember what one looks like in detail? Very few people can. This simple exercise helps us sharpen our observational skills and shows how easy it is to overlook the objects of everyday life:

1. *Describe a penny.* Without looking at one, write a detailed description of both sides of a penny. Take your time. Close your eyes and visualize. Do the best you can.

2. *Explore what you missed.* When you have come up with the best description possible, compare it to an actual penny. Pay attention to what you missed and what you got correct. Did you see the overall pattern but miss details? Did you identify specifics but forget how they were all put together? Were there certain things that you were sure were on the coin, that were not? These patterns of remembering and forgetting can tell us much about what we pay attention to and what we do not.

3. *Use other objects.* Try writing descriptions of other common things without looking at them. Can you describe the pattern on your kitchen curtains, the locations and kinds of plants in front of a building you visit often? Can you describe the gas station you go to every week or the cover of a book you have had in your house for

many years? Give these descriptions a try and then use the results to develop your attentiveness.

—————————————{ SACRED TOOL }—————————————

Watching a Stone

When entomologist Samuel Scudder was first studying under the renowned scientist Louis Agassiz, he was ordered to observe a single dead fish and report the most obvious fact about it. What Scudder expected to take a few minutes required many days of observation and many attempts to come up with the correct answer—until he finally realized that it was simply the fact that the fish had two identical sides.[5] Scudder's story proves a frequently overlooked point: the hardest thing to truly pay attention to is something familiar to us. If Scudder had never seen a fish before, he would certainly have spotted the fish's conspicuous symmetry right away, but his familiarity kept him from even noticing it. This story also teaches us the importance of sustained attention: Scudder stared at his fish for days before he solved Agassiz's riddle. How good are your observational skills? How long can you focus on a common object? You can find out by watching something very familiar—a simple stone:

1. *Prepare to observe a stone.* Pick an ordinary stone. Don't go for something particularly colorful or interesting. An unremarkable stone will do. Place it in a quiet area where you won't be disturbed. Set a timer for twenty minutes. Sit comfortably and watch your stone.

2. *Employ all your senses.* You may use all your senses to observe the stone—smell it, touch it, weigh it in your hand—but mainly you will want to watch it.

3. *Stick with it*. After a minute or two, you will decide that you have observed everything there is about the stone. Keep watching. A minute or so later, you will start to feel bored, and that boredom will soon become intense. Keep observing. At some point you may begin to feel that this is the stupidest exercise you've ever done and if you stare at that stone for one more minute, you're liable to do something rash. You may start blaming the stone for being so boring. You may even begin to hate it. Keep watching, keep watching, keep watching. At some point, often quite suddenly, the stone will seem to open in front of your eyes. You will see things in it that eluded you at first. The plain gray rock will suddenly reveal an astounding array of colors. Its texture will display its true complexity. The beauty of its ordinary, asymmetrical shape will emerge.

4. *Write*. Only after you've experienced that opening will you be ready. Once you are, take pen in hand and write. Describe everything you saw in the stone, everything you perceived through your other senses. Describe the feelings you went through as you watched the stone. If you find your writing going off onto something else, you can choose to follow that path or to bring your writing quietly back to the stone and delve deeper into it. However you write, do it with a sense of freedom and openness.

Wu Wei

Stemming from ancient Chinese philosophy, especially Taoist thought, *wu wei* literally means *without action*. It refers to being in tune with the Universe, to a kind of spontaneous, natural, and accepting way of living that can be called *effortless action* or *creative stillness*. *Wu wei* is based on the notion that the Tao—the mysterious All or Cosmic Unity of which we are all a part— is constantly changing and evolving and that fighting that continual flux is unhealthy, detrimental, and ultimately fruitless. It tells us to "go with the flow," to act without effort, and to stop our never-ending struggle to create the perfect existence that always eludes us.

Wu wei means knowing when to act and when not to act, listening to nature, synchronicity, intuition, our bodies. It teaches us to act with detachment, without striving for specific results. The result isn't a state of total passivity or weakness, but a kind of power that is fluid, subtle, and invisible. In the same way, we allow our feelings and experiences to come and go without fighting them. We learn to perceive the Tao in all things, allow it to work through us, and align ourselves with it.

—————————————————{ SACRED TOOL }———————————————————

Writing from Not Knowing

"Write what you know!" is advice that most writers have heard a thousand times (and that many good writers ignore). Knowing is, of course, the work of the rational part of your mind. To access the nonrational realm, we need to write from not knowing. In Zen, this is sometimes called *beginner's mind*. It can also be thought of as *child's mind*. Beginners and children start with a fresh slate. They don't make all sorts of assumptions based on prior knowledge. They keep their eyes open and their imaginations free. Try writing from this place, empty of knowledge, answers, and preconceptions:

1. *Pick something you don't know.* It shouldn't be hard to find something: Do you know how a computer stores memory, how a car works, or a refrigerator? Do you know how people in the Hunan Province of China farm or how the Arawak people of the Amazon build their houses? Do you know how monarch butterflies get from Minnesota to Mexico, how and where your mattress was manufactured, the route your Chilean strawberries took to get to your supermarket in

Lincoln, Nebraska? Perhaps you know all of those things, but there are surely other things you don't know. In fact, it's often rather discouraging to realize how little we know about the world.

2. *Write like a child.* Rather than letting it get us down, we can use not knowing as a source of creativity. Once you have picked something you don't know, write about it. How can you write about it when you don't know? You do it the way a child does it. Children know very little about the world, yet they can often "explain" how something works, and their explanations are sometimes very ingenious. How *might* a butterfly get to Mexico from the Midwest? If you already know, then there is only one possibility. If you don't know, the possibilities are infinite. Go with those possibilities and let your imagination soar.

───────────────{ SACRED TOOL }───────────────

Welcoming Failure

Going with the flow in the Taoist sense means working without the feeling that we must see results, achievements, and successes. It makes failure as acceptable as success because they are both part of the incessant flow of the Tao. This attitude requires a very steady nature—and usually many years of meditation—but having even a sliver of it is a great boon to writers because almost all of us experience considerable failure in our lives. Imagine how good it would feel to be able to respond to failure as just another experience—no better or worse than success. Perhaps that is too much to ask for from most of us, but we can take a step in that direction by reframing failure and thinking about it in fresh ways. There are a number of writing exercises that can help us foster that attitude:

1. *Recalling desires that became disappointments.* Think of a time when something you wanted very badly and finally achieved turned out to be a great disappointment. Most of us have gone through this at one time or other. At last, you get that ideal job you've been searching for, only to discover that it is far more exhausting, frustrating, and stressful than you ever imagined. You're overjoyed at finally winning the heart of someone you've been interested in for years, then discover that he isn't the person you thought he was. Many writers who yearn to get a book published discover that this supreme goal doesn't bring the money, fame, or sense of achievement they expected. Go back in your life and see if you can find some examples of this all-too-common experience.

2. *Write the desire.* Think deeply about what you expected that experience to be. Put yourself back into the daydream you had when you were in the longing stage. Try to relive what you were feeling. Then write. Detail the "perfect" day you thought you would have on that new job or with that special person. What did you expect to gain—an end to loneliness, a sense of security, a chance to show up those who doubted you? Write about that feeling with all the delight and cheer you expected.

3. *Write the disappointment.* Now relive the way the experience actually turned out. Let yourself stew a little: go back into that stress, disappointment, or disillusionment. Feel it deeply. Then write about it, drawing from all the anger, grief, and regret you felt.

4. *Compare.* When you are finished, compare the two versions. Don't despair over the fact that things didn't turn out the way you expected—when do they ever? Instead, see this as a perfect example of the fact that we don't really have that much control over our destinies and the amount of energy we put into grasping for things is often ill spent.

Drawing Success from Failure

This exercise is the mirror image of the previous one. In this one, we look at something we saw as a terrible disappointment that turned out to be a positive experience:

1. *Write the grief.* Recall the sense of grief, frustration, and anger you felt at your frustrated wishes. Remember what you told yourself then. Were you stuck in a "poor me" mode, thinking things like, "I'm such a loser. Nothing good ever happens to me"? Or were you really ticked off and dreaming of revenge? When you have thoroughly immersed yourself in those feelings of self-pity, anger, bitterness, or grief, write about them.

2. *Write the joy.* Now turn to the happiness and pride that supplanted those negative feelings. Let yourself rejoice with that success just as thoroughly and deeply as you wallowed in the failure. Write about that joy—and let out all the stops. One writer wrote about the deep shame she had brought her conservative family when she gave birth as an unmarried teenager, and then about the child who grew into a lovely person, her best friend, and the deepest source of joy in her life. Another woman wrote about her disappointment when, because of her husband's work, she had to turn down a job at a top-notch law firm for a less prestigious one in another city. In this part of the exercise, she wrote about how she and her new employer suddenly shot to fame with a particularly noteworthy case she would have missed if she'd taken the more prestigious job. You may not have had such a dramatic experience, but most of us at one time or another have seen failures turn into unexpected successes.

Like the previous exercise, this one makes us realize that "going with the flow" of things is often the best thing we can do. Since we can't control everything that happens to us, sometimes all we can do is practice acceptance. And besides, we never know how things are going to turn out: leave well enough alone, and they may fall into place on their own.

{ SACRED TOOL }

Turning Mistakes into Tools

Another way to practice *wu wei* is to use our omissions or errors as gateways to new paths. This means paying attention to the times we get things wrong and, rather than quickly trying to repair the mistake, following it to its logical conclusion. There is no set way to do this, but some examples can give an idea of how it works:

1. *Using minor errors.* One writer struggled with what to name the characters in her novel. She finally settled on Johanna for one of them, but she didn't feel it was quite right. As she was rereading a chapter, she discovered a typo: she'd written "Lohanna" by accident. Suddenly, she had a new name for her character, one that captured the character's colorful and slightly eccentric personality.

2. *Replacing lost work with better work.* Before the days of computers, one writer found his half-written novel soaked after a water pipe in his apartment broke. Although he managed to save some of the pages, dry them out, and use them, many were destroyed, leaving significant gaps in his work. After ranting, cursing, and wallowing in self-pity for a while, he went to work, leaving out material he'd once felt was indispensable, and rewriting other missing parts in

completely new ways. The result, he felt, was a stronger, more vivid, and deeper work than the first version.

3. *Saving your darlings.* Many writers have had the experience of "killing their darlings"—something you may have experienced when an editor, or your own inner voice, tells you a passage you love needs to be omitted. This is especially painful if you worked for many days honing the passage into what seemed like perfection. Rather than erasing the passage entirely, save it. Put it in an envelope with all your other omitted passages or in a different folder on your computer. Later, go back to the eliminated passage and use it to start an entirely new piece. What was a flaw in the first work might turn out to be a gem in the new one.

Mistakes have all the ingredients for crazy wisdom: they are serendipitous and unplanned, and they often give us unexpected insights. Develop a new attitude toward your mistakes. Instead of viewing them as bad or shameful things, see them as doors to new vistas. Treasure them and care for them. You may find some rich material in gaffes, accidents, and failures.

—————————————{ SACRED TOOL }—————————————

Emptying Out

For this exercise, use something you've already written, either recently or some time ago. You can work on something as small as a short paragraph or as long as an entire short story, depending on how much time you wish to put into the exercise, but a medium-sized passage seems to work best for most writers:

1. *Read the work.* Begin by reading the work aloud. Get a sense of its rhythm and melody, of what you feel works and doesn't work in it,

but don't be too judgmental—work from the go-with-the-flow mentality of *wu wei*.

2. *Eliminate adverbs*. Make a copy of the work you've chosen to use for this exercise so that you keep the original unchanged. Now go through the passage and eliminate *all* adverbs. Don't worry about whether the word changes the meaning of a sentence—it rarely does—or whether it's a really great adverb that you want to keep. Simply wipe all adverbs away. Keep in mind that adverbs take many forms and are easy to miss: you might catch "speedily," "especially," and "dauntingly," but don't forget "often," "many," "very," "too," and the other small adverbs that crop up like weeds in our work. If you need to remind yourself of the many forms adverbs take, consult a good handbook on English grammar or a grammar website. Another thing you can do is replace adverb-verb combinations with stronger verbs whenever possible, so that "He walked quickly to the door" becomes "He rushed," "He flew," or "He scrambled."

3. *Read the work*. When you are certain that all of your adverbs are gone, read the passage aloud again. How has it changed? You will almost always find that it seems sharper and clearer and has a subtle power that the previous version lacked.

4. *Eliminate adjectives*. Now do the same thing for adjectives, again ridding your work of every one. These words are less insidious than adverbs: they are more noticeable and don't muddy up our prose as much as their adverbial cousins. But most of them can be eliminated without changing the meaning of a sentence and, even if they do, get rid of them for the time being.

5. *Read the passage aloud again*. Pay attention to how it has changed.

6. *Eliminate deadwood.* Now do a third revision, this time getting rid of anything else that just doesn't need to be there. Ask yourself for each clause you come to, "Does the passage absolutely need this?" If you can't answer with a confident "Yes!" then eliminate it. Going through a fourth time to make sure you've caught these is also a good idea.

7. *Revise.* At this point, you have cut your passage down to its core. You have gotten rid of deadweight words and obese sentences, decoration and flamboyance, and what you have left is as simple and pure as a Zen meditation hall. It will almost certainly be far cleaner and incisive than the passage you began with. And it will have the kind of subtle, quiet power that can knock a reader's socks off. This does not mean, however, that you won't want to go back and replace some of the elements you eliminated. Some of them will be necessary and beneficial. But after cleaning your work out in this way, you will be able to see much more clearly which extra words are needed and which are not.

———•·•·•———

Writers deal with things that can't be solved or managed through reason and logic: emotions, relationships, insights, memories. We explore a world not of clear-cut answers and simple solutions, but one of paradox, confusion, and incongruity. The mysterious and paradoxical are our stock in trade.

Crazy wisdom allows us to rest comfortably with uncertainty, ambiguity, and doubt, to accept the mysteries and enigmas of life instead of desperately reaching after facts and logic. These exercises give us the chance to play with riddles and puzzles, to wander through unsolvable mysteries, and to expand our horizons beyond the walls of reason out to the infinite reaches of the imagination.

If this all seems too ethereal and outlandish, rest easy. In the next part, we will explore the much more down-to-earth world of the monastery. From the mystic, we have discovered how to open to the All. The monk can teach us how to live simply and harmoniously in the everyday world. The next two chapters will explore ways to learn from the monk's basic, deeply effective practice of silence and solitude and from his everyday experience of life in community with others.

PART II | *The Monastic Path*

In *The Monastic Journey*, Thomas Merton writes about "special groups of men and women who separate themselves from the ordinary life of society, take upon themselves particular and difficult obligations, and devote themselves to one task above all: to deepening their understanding and practice of their own religion in its most basic implications."[1] Merton is describing the life of the monk in this passage, but if we substitute the word "writing" for "religion"—and it is not a far-fetched trade—then his words depict the writer's life as well.

Of course, a list of monastic qualities would hardly appear to fit most writers. We avoid poverty whenever possible, engage in manual labor only when we have to, and are disinclined to be celibate—and anyone who knows a few of us would laugh out loud at the suggestion that we cultivate humility. The majority of us live in ordinary homes, have families, and work for pay, and as a group, we can hardly make claims of saintliness.

Nonetheless, correspondences between the monastic world and the writing life run deep beneath the differences. Like monks, writers have a yearning for truth and a relentless desire to find meaning in the world. We are willing to forego many of the pleasures of the world for our art, and we frequently work without expecting pay or recognition. We, too, know the importance of contemplation, and at our best, we show a monklike discipline and devotion.

Monks are expert in many qualities writers emulate. They are utterly committed to their path and they labor, not for material gain, but for the intrinsic value of their work. They know the importance of silence, simplicity, and submission to something larger than themselves. They accept the role they play on the outskirts of conventional society. To develop the ability to write with constancy and sureness even when our work has not yet brought us the kind of success we would like, to write with utter dedication and the willingness to work hard, to experience the value of silence and solitude while continuing to take part in our families and community—for help with these, writers can turn to the monks' millennia of experience.

The Writer in Silence and Solitude

OF ALL THE QUALITIES valued by writers and monks alike, the most essential are probably silence and solitude. These twin blessings are the essence of all monastic traditions. The Buddhist forest monk meditating in the dense woodlands of Thailand, the wandering Hindu *saddhu* who renounces all contact with society, the desert hermit of early Christianity, and the modern Catholic monk all know the power of silence and solitude. They are equally essential to the writer's work. "Writing is something you do alone in a room," writes essayist Michael Ventura. "Before any issues of style, content or form can be addressed, the fundamental question is: How long can you stay in that room?"[1] Virginia Woolf made a similar point in her seminal essay, "A Room of One's Own," in which she argued, among other things, that one of the essential requirements for literary creation is a place to be alone.[2] Poet Marguerite Duras put it more dramatically: without solitude, she said, "writing would crumble, drained bloodless."[3]

One of the greatest blessings of silence and solitude is that they help us identify and break through old practices. It is easy to start relying on familiar patterns and habits in our writing. We have signature ways of forming sentences, using words, employing imagery, and so on. We reuse the same rhythms, the same metaphors, the same transitions, beginnings, and endings. We rely on them and frequently use them because we've heard them so many times. When your mind is constantly busy, it has no time to develop fresh techniques. Silence and solitude allow us to create a clear, wide space in our minds—like a wind that blows the clouds away, leaving an expanse of blue. With the old ingrained ways of doing things swept aside, all sorts of new things can grow.

Another gift of silence and solitude is their ability to bring us in touch with the mythic, nonrational awareness all human beings are born with. The conventional world keeps us using the logical parts of our minds: we need reason to organize, plan, and remember all the things we are called on to do. But writing moves beyond rational thinking into a greater knowing. Mythic consciousness gives deep meaning to the experiences of our lives. It enables us to see ourselves as part of a greater whole and to tap into a more profound understanding of the patterns of existence. It is tied to the root experiences of human beings, which make up the material we write from. In solitude, we can shut off the logic and reason that we need to function in daily life and allow mythic consciousness to appear, giving us remarkably clear, deep awareness.

Silence and solitude allow us to discover our authentic selves, develop a mature discipline, increase our self-reliance, and simply rest. Unfortunately, they are not easy to come by. It takes time and effort to seek them out and cultivate them. But once we find a place for them in our lives, we immediately realize how much we've been missing without them.

Fostering Silence and Solitude

It is impossible in our noisy, crowded times to imagine the silence experienced by the desert hermits of early Christianity or Hindu holy men living high in the Himalayas. Most of us don't have deserts or remote mountain passes to wander in, and, even if we did, our responsibilities would keep us from spending much time there. Instead, we must find ways to nurture silence and solitude in the midst of our busy schedules. The most basic way to do this is simply creating space for them—not merely reducing noise or finding time away from others, but creating a state in which our inner voices are stilled and we stand alone with the Mystery.

———————————————{ SACRED TOOL }———————————————

Sitting with Silence

Basically, the only way we can foster silence and solitude are to make room for them in our lives—and then learn to deal with them when we've found them. Here is one structured way of creating an opening for silence and solitude:

1. *Find the setting.* Discover a place and time where you can be fairly assured that you will not be bothered. Of course, a two-week silent retreat would be lovely, but most of us will be lucky to find a half hour when the family is out of the house. Even if all you can manage is ten minutes twice a week when everyone else is asleep, take it. It will still have an effect on your writing, and as it becomes part of your writing practice, you may find ways to expand it.

2. *Set an interval.* It is important to know ahead of time how long you expect to sit in silence. Depending on how well you tolerate doing nothing, you might make it anywhere from ten minutes to an hour

or longer, but make sure you know from the beginning when your interval of silence will end. Otherwise, you are likely to stop it as soon as you get restless, rather than challenging yourself to wait through the boredom and impatience.

3. *Make the place truly silent.* This means quieting both physical and mental noise. Wait until you have the house, or at least a room, to yourself. Unplug the phone. Don't answer the door, check your email, read, or go online. Make the time not just absent of noise, but absent of busyness. Don't use it to clean house, pay bills, plan your week, knit, or doodle. You may plan to write when your silent time is over, but only after you've sat with silence for a while.

4. *Move if you wish.* If you want, you can do some kind of slow, quiet movement. If you do yoga or tai chi, they are perfect silent practices. Walking slowly also works. But as you're moving, don't forget about the silence around you. Don't get lost in other thoughts.

5. *Be comfortable.* If you aren't going to engage in some kind of silent movement, sit in the posture you assume for meditation—neither rigid nor slumping, but comfortable. Don't lie down unless you want to substitute sleeping for sitting in silence. Spend a moment centering yourself through deep breathing.

6. *Simply sit.* Rest in the silence. Don't fidget, don't do anything special. There's no need to concentrate on anything or practice deep breathing. Don't try to focus on the breath, a mantra, or any other type of meditational object. Simply be aware of the silence. Let yourself feel whatever comes up in this open space.

7. *Accept intrusive noises.* You will immediately discover that your silence isn't truly silent. You will probably hear *something*. Traffic from far away. The distant bark of a dog. The rain against your

window or the creaking of the floorboards. Accept the faint noises that intrude into your silence. Consider them part of the silence, rather than interference.

8. *Don't write*. This is the hardest part for writers: don't write—not even in your head. Writers are often shocked at this suggestion. It's difficult to refrain from writing when you want to write and have the time right then to do it. You may get edgy sitting there with nothing to do and your notebook just a few feet away. As the minutes pass, that desire may turn into an irresistible craving. Resist it. Why? Because when you are writing, you are not experiencing silence. You are writing. To gain the benefits of silence, you must rest in it, focus your awareness on it, listen to it. Only through awareness can you gain the benefits that silence brings.

9. *Write*. When your scheduled silent time is over, write from the stillness that has grown inside you. Let the words come of their own accord from that still center. If you feel yourself losing the quiet core you accessed earlier, stop for a moment, breathe deeply, and simply recall how you felt sitting in silence. Continue writing.

You may find that what you write after you have sat silently for a while is markedly different from your usual work. By focusing on the silence, you have given your mind the opportunity to open and expand. Without trying, you have reached a new level where your old patterns can fall away. But if you don't see a difference in your writing, don't worry. Keep up a regular silence practice, and you will eventually see its effects on your writing—and your life.

Turning Aside

The practice of *turning aside* is an invaluable tool for the writer. Developed by Wayne Edward Oates—the renowned psychologist who coined the term *workaholic*—it means looking away from the turbulence around you to some small, quiet thing.[4] Practiced any time you are in a hectic place, this easy exercise can bring an internal quiet even in the midst of chaos:

1. *Turn aside.* The next time you find yourself in a crowd, focus for one moment on some small thing. In the crush of a department store, spend a moment watching a little girl holding a doll. On a packed commuter train, focus on the play of light on the windows. Stuck in traffic amid short-tempered drivers and blaring horns, glance upward to see the clouds moving across the sky. In this way, you can find solitude and silence in the busiest of places.

2. *Study the noise.* The next time you write, use the experience as an exercise in contrast and balance. Spend a few moments reliving the noise and bustle you found yourself in. Recall the sounds and sights, the sense of crowding or confusion, the frantic or panicky feeling you may have had. Allow yourself to wallow for a moment in those sensory images and emotions. Now create a series of metaphors expressing those oppressive or anxious feelings. Do this as a speed writing exercise, coming up with as many metaphors as you can in a minute or two.

3. *Study the turning-aside moment.* When you have come up with as many metaphors as you can, relax for a moment, and then go through the same process for the turning-aside moment. Relive the experience. Allow the sense of relief to settle over you as you recall

the details of the scene you turned to. Let the noise grow dim and the tension and sense of crowding disappear. Rest for a moment in the tranquility of turning aside. Now go back to the list of metaphors you came up with earlier. For each metaphor that captured the sense of noise and crowding, find one that contrasts, expressing the peaceful, centered feeling of turning aside. You might come up with something like this:

Noisy Place	Quiet Scene
A flock of geese honking in the sky	A single swan on a lake
The taste of sharp cheddar	The flavor of fresh cream
The feeling of barbed wire	The feeling of cotton yarn
A double espresso	A cup of chamomile tea

The possibilities are endless—and will be very different from writer to writer. Play with it.

5. *Write a poem.* Another way to use the experience is to create a poem about what you focused on when you turned away from the noise and chaos. Often, turning toward something brings our attention to its fine details and helps us see its essence. When we turn from the blaring horns and short tempers of a traffic jam to a flock of blackbirds flying overhead or the frost crystals forming on a window, we often see those things with a special kind of sharp awareness. This can make for rich, effective poetry.

6. *Use it as a grounding device.* You can use the memory of your turning-aside experience as a grounding device. When you find yourself getting anxious, blocked, or scattered as you write, mentally return to that moment of turning aside. You will find yourself immediately feeling calmer.

Developing Self-Sufficiency

The Buddhist scriptures tell us, "Look within: Thou art the Buddha." The Christian tradition says, "The Kingdom of Heaven is within you." The only thing we really need, to get in touch with the Mystery, is ourselves. For the writer, this type of profound self-reliance and self-trust are indispensable. But we can only achieve them when we are away from the opinions of friends, teachers, and editors, the manipulation of advertisements and shop windows, the influence of "conventional wisdom." The only way we can get away from those things is through solitude. Freedom from the effects of communal persuasion is only found when we remove ourselves from community.

But even when we are alone, the attitudes and expectations of others shadow us. It takes work to shed the years of relying on other people to validate us. These exercises can help us over that barrier and lead us toward true self-sufficiency.

{ SACRED TOOL }

Surviving in the Desert

Buddhist forest monks and early Christian hermits had wild places where they could live alone for many years. Most of us don't. But we can create a wild place in our minds and then develop the mental self-reliance to survive there:

1. *Embark on a solitary journey*. Imagine that you are going off to be alone in a wild setting: a forest, a desert, or a remote mountain pass, perhaps. You must leave behind the people and things you normally rely on. Don't panic: you are not leaving them for good. You are merely going on a sojourn and will soon return. But for this journey, you must learn to depend only on yourself.

2. *Show gratitude.* Think of all the people you depend on, especially those who support your writing: anyone who gives you reassurance, who willingly reads your work to tell you what they think, who comforts you when your stories or poems are rejected, who offers gentle but honest critiques, who provides wise advice. As you mentally walk into that forest or desert, see yourself coming upon each of them one by one. Each time you do, imagine thanking the person for all they've done, explaining that you must be on your own for a time, and telling them you will return. Leave each one behind as you continue walking.

3. *Go as far as you can.* When you are fully alone in the wilderness of your imagination, keep walking. You need to be as far away as you can reasonably go to truly learn self-sufficiency. When you have gone as far as your imagination will take you and feel confident that you have truly left your familiar support system behind, rest in that place. Let the sense of being completely alone—and dependent on no one but yourself—sink into your bones.

4. *Review your needs.* Think of all the things you will need to survive in the place you have chosen. Shelter and protection from the cold might be among the first things to think about. Food and water are certainly high on the list. You will need fire for warmth and to cook with, and you will need a way to prepare food. You might also need something with which to fend off wild animals. Will you also need a knowledge of local plants to distinguish which are edible, poisonous, or medicinal? Will you need something to sleep on, something to keep you dry or protect you from the sun?

5. *Identify your resources.* For a writer exploring her own self-sufficiency, what might these things consist of? This is where you need to look deep within to discover the resources you may not even know you

have. What serves as shelter to the writer on her own? What is her sustenance, her fire, her bedding? Think hard and be creative. Write them out in sentences, "My shelter is . . . ," "My food is. . . ." One writer came up with this list:

→ My shelter is dancing. Every time I get up and dance or go to my dance class, I feel as if I am creating a bubble around me that nothing bad can penetrate. It can keep me safe from the "cold and rain" that sometimes hit me when I'm too blocked to write.

→ My food is my imagination. It is the one thing I feel I am truly gifted at, and it nourishes me. If it weren't for my ability to let my imagination go, I would never survive the writing life.

→ My water is sleep. When I wake up in the morning—or after a nap—I feel like I've been purified, cleansed, and refreshed.

→ My protection again the fierce beasts of the jungle is my ability to deal with failure. Even though it hurts whenever I get a rejection, I am pretty good at bouncing back and getting back to work.

→ My cooking tools are the skills I've built from writing poetry for ten years. They help me transform words into poems the way an oven would help me transform raw grain into bread.

Avoid bringing others into this exercise, as in, "My sister is my shelter, always there to make me feel better." This is not because you want to diminish your appreciation for the people who have helped you along the way, but because the focus of this particular exercise is *you* and the sources of strength and courage you have inside.

Opening to the Shadows

Silence and solitude are not all restfulness and bliss. Acoustics designer Michael Stocker has pointed out that silence can be uncomfortable when it makes us feel insignificant,[5] and Wayne Oates writes that the small voices we hear in silence may seem dark and evil.[6] Our first impulse when the silence becomes too frightening is to end it: hurry off to the mall, call a friend, or turn on the TV. Sometimes turning back is the best action; sometimes fighting your fears is better. But there are times when we should embrace the darkness, and there are ways we can deal with the darker side of solitude without running away.

{ SACRED TOOL }

Listening to the Mystery

Psychiatrist Jacques Castermane says silence is disturbing because it is a "door opening to mystery."[7] When we are away from the noise of everyday life, we have the opportunity to hear the great voice that permeates the Universe. We can call it the voice of the Void. It is not easy listening to that vast and mysterious voice—it can be terrifying. But we must allow ourselves to hear it if we want to grow spiritually and creatively. Rather than shattering the silence, this exercise has us face it:

1. *Sit in solitude*. Center yourself and settle into the silence. When you feel centered, visualize yourself in a very solitary place: a mountaintop, a desert, a deserted island—anywhere that you can imagine yourself entirely alone. Make the place vivid. See, hear, and smell it. Allow yourself to *be* in that place.

2. *See the voice.* Visualize the dark and mysterious something. You can see it as a shadow cast by some invisible thing, or it might be a cloud or wind or some other indistinct, inscrutable form. Watch it approach slowly.

3. *Allow it to speak through you.* When the voice is before you, say nothing. Instead, write. Allow it to speak through your pen or keyboard. Its words may be simple, soothing, shocking, or incomprehensible. It doesn't matter. Let it speak. You will know when it has finished: when you have written all you can.

4. *Allow it to retreat.* Put your pen down and wait. Allow the voice time to move away. Watch it disappear.

5. *Read the words of the voice.* Read what you have written with the gentle intention of understanding it. That is, contemplate it, but without straining. Don't think, "I need to figure out what this means! I must!" Instead, allow the meaning to come to you when it will. If it doesn't at first, set it aside for another day. Keep the words of the voice and reread them each day—but only when you've been sitting in silence for a while, so your mind will be open to mythic meaning. Eventually, the message will become clear.

ALLOWING CREATIVE ENERGY TO RISE FROM SILENCE

Our minds yearn to be busy. When we are with others, we occupy ourselves watching, listening to, communicating with, and responding to those around us. This is healthy and normal—as long as we know when to withdraw. Constant preoccupation with the day-to-day affairs of the world sets up a giant roadblock in the way of our creativity. When we are with others, we are merrily dancing in the world of busyness and activity. It is when we are alone that we venture into the realm of imagination.

If you meditate, you know how productive the human brain is. Even advanced meditators find their minds wandering off onto all sorts of topics. This is because we are all part of the creative force of the Universe. In our natural state, our minds are continually spinning and weaving. This natural creativity erupts most powerfully when we are alone. Without the distractions of work, entertainment, and other people, our lifelines to the creative centers of the Universe engage, and up bubble all kinds of magical things. Put another way, solitude takes us away from the tumult of daily life and allows our inborn creativity—which is one with the great creative force of the Universe—to flow.

Unfortunately, we are often so enmeshed in the day-to-day world that even when we steal a few moments of silence, it can be difficult to still our minds enough for that natural creativity to come through. Certain techniques can help us overcome these barriers.

---------------------------{ SACRED TOOL }---------------------------

Experiencing Metamorphosis

Few images depict growth and development more vividly than that of the humble caterpillar turning into a butterfly. It is such an apt metaphor—from creeping to flying, from wormlike to lovely—that it has become trite from overuse. It taps into the same emotional forces that lead us to curl up under quilts when we need rest or recovery, pull the blanket over our heads when we want a feeling of protection, and build forts or tents to hide in when we are children. Those coverings offer us darkness and quiet, comfort and safety; they muffle the outside world and give us a place to be with ourselves, just as a cocoon does.

Despite being overused, the cocoon can be a powerful image to invoke when you want to encourage the rise of creative energy. Devising—or just imagining—a cocoon can provide a special kind of solitude, veiling you from the affairs of the world in your own separate space:

1. *Create a cocoon.* After you have rested in silence for a while, create a cocoon. You may simply visualize the cocoon, picturing the fine threads winding around and around you, until you are resting comfortably inside them, separated from the world, but some writers actually create a physical cocoon from a blanket or other covering. If you dance or enjoy movement, you can dance or mime the creation of a cocoon, the withdrawal into a separate space.

2. *Rest there.* However you evoke the feeling of being in a cocoon, rest inside it. Don't try to make anything happen—that will just chase your creative impulse away. Instead, picture your creativity growing within the cocoon. If you don't want to mix metaphors, you might see it as colorful wings, but it can be anything—a sprouting seed, a flowering tree, the rise of energy from the base of your spine through your body. Give it time, let it grow, and allow it to build up until you can't wait any longer.

3. *Emerge and write.* When you feel ready, emerge. Use the image you have developed in your cocoon as a catalyst for your imagination. Open your wings, allow the flowers to spread their seeds, feel the energy flowing from your spine down your fingers. Write whatever you wish—a project you have already begun, something totally new, or a free-flowing meditation. Write with an awareness of the beautiful flowering you have experienced.

Becoming Your Authentic Self

One of the great blessings of solitude and silence is that they offer time for us to become who we really are. They take us away from the demands and obligations others lay on us and give us relief from the constant pull in all directions by employers, family members, friends, and the many kinds of folderol modern life has created. They allow us respite from the modern burden of multitasking. The constant need to meet the expectations of others draws writers away from their true selves and deafens us to our authentic voices. You can't remember who you are when half the world is vying for your attention: you need solitude for that.

Although simply sitting with the silence can aid our journey to authenticity, there are also a number of techniques you can specifically use to explore who you are. These techniques make use of the opening up of intuition and awareness that occurs when we rest with silence and solitude.

---------------------------------{ SACRED TOOL }---------------------------------

Removing the Mask

This multipart exercise can be done just once or repeated many times, going deeper with each repetition:

1. *Describe yourself.* Begin with the sitting-in-silence practice described earlier, but this time, at the end of your silent period, write a description of yourself. Include whatever details seem pertinent and don't reject anything. It is best to set a time limit—five, ten, or twenty minutes, perhaps—or a maximum number of pages. This will keep your description down to the bare bones, which often brings the more important issues to the fore. When you are finished, read what you have written. If you remember something new and essential

as you read, add it, but don't go overboard: you want to keep the description lean.

The depiction you have just come up with can be thought of as your "mask." It may be the face you wear for the world to see, but, more importantly, it's what *you* believe. If you've worn that mask long enough, you will have bought into it yourself: when you look in the mirror, you see the mask, rather than your true face.

2. *Explore your description.* Now read what you wrote a second time. This time, for each statement you have made about yourself ask, "Am I really this?" You may ask the question aloud or write it down, "Am I really a hothead with a bad temper?" "Am I really gentle and kind-hearted?" "Am I truly interested in studying architecture?" Don't dwell on the answer. A spontaneous expression—before your rational brain interferes—will be the truest. Each time you answer no to the question "Am I really this?," put a line through the statement on your page.

3. *Break open the statements you rejected.* When you have gone through the entire description, go back and read all the statements you put a line through. Chances are these are things that other people believe you are or want you to be. You've always been told you would make a good nurse—but is that really what you want to do? Your parents used to praise you for being so polite, but maybe you were really seething inside every time you said, "Thank you." You might even answer no to something that seems like an inalienable part of you, as in, "No, I am not thirty-two years old." What could that mean? That you aren't where you think you should be at thirty-two? That you are not as mature as other people your age? That you are wise beyond your years? That you refuse to be defined by age? If you want, you can go through a second level of weeding out, crossing out still

more statements. As you challenge the things you've thought of as yourself, you will be breaking off pieces of the mask you have been wearing.

4. *Look for the source.* For each statement you rejected, ask yourself where the idea came from. If you can identify the source, write it down next to or below the statement: "I know this—it started when my tenth-grade coach told me I was a lousy baseball player" or "This came from my parents' wish that I become an engineer." If you can't figure out where the idea came from, that is all right, too—we can't always sort through the thousands of things that have influenced our identities over a lifetime.

5. *Highlight the core description.* By *core description* we mean the statements you *didn't* reject. Look at them with fresh eyes: they are probably the closest you can come right now to identifying your authentic self. If it helps, write them again on a clean sheet of paper, leaving behind the crossed-out ones.

What you will probably arrive at through this process is a much truer description of yourself than you started out with. You may be astonished at how skewed your thinking about yourself has been. Your mask has almost become a part of you—it may have adhered to the face underneath so that removal must be done slowly and carefully so as not to tear the skin. But, as painful as removing the mask may be, you may also feel a deep sense of relief that you've moved away from that imposed self to the true self underneath.

SILENCE AS REST

We have discussed ways that solitude and silence can be used to develop self-sufficiency, creativity, authenticity, and awareness. But these two blessings don't always have to be the sources of change and achievement. The most basic thing they offer the writer—and the monk—is rest. Over three hundred years ago, William Penn wrote, "True silence . . . is to the spirit what sleep is to the body, nourishment and refreshment."[8] His statement is even truer in this hurried age. If you work at a stressful job, take care of a busy family, or are overwhelmed with your commitments, you may be depleting the energy you need to write. Time alone in silence can give us a chance to recover and refresh ourselves.

{ SACRED TOOL }

Resting

This exercise requires that you be kind to yourself, set aside deadlines, and relax your own self-imposed rules:

1. *Shed expectations.* When you have found your time and place for silence, go there without expecting anything. Don't say to yourself, "Great—I have a whole half hour to charge up my batteries." Instead, forget about the pressure of time.

2. *Don't worry.* Stop fretting about the fact that you're not writing, that you don't feel particularly productive, that your creativity seems to be hibernating. Maybe you aren't ready right now to invoke your creativity or delve into the depths of your soul. Allow yourself that space. Breathe. Let go. Just be. For five minutes of your life, do not try to accomplish anything.

"Writers must be comfortable with aloneness; free of guilt at delight in our own company," writes poet Donald M. Murray. "We must find our own way to achieve quiet so that we can hear the whisper of the emerging text."[9] This solitude and silence are as essential to the writing life as any tool or technique. Unfortunately, they are not easily found. Unlike monks, writers have to fight for them—carve out niches, create our own separate spaces, find ways to quell the noise and busyness of the world. Then we can still ourselves, and listen. "That," says Murray, "is where it all begins, alone."[10]

Silence and solitude are what we most often think of when we visualize the life of the monk, but if we imagine the monastic life to be all solitary contemplation, we are seeing only half the picture. The paradox of the monastic life is that, as much as it stresses standing alone before the Mystery, it rests on communal living—just as the writer's life is built on families, friends, and communities. We learned a great deal about ways of being alone from the monastic's experience. In the next chapter, we'll learn about ways of being with others.

{6}

The Writer in Community

WRITERS MAY FIND their voices in solitude, but their work grows out of the busy, crowded life of family, workplace, and community. Being with others is the complementary piece of the puzzle, as crucial to good writing as time spent alone. "You must live in the outer world," Dylan Thomas wrote to his friend, novelist Pamela Hansford. "Suffer in it and with it, enjoy its changes, despair at them. . . . You *have* to do that."[1]

The writer can learn much about the blessings and trials of communal life from the monastery. Monks of all traditions are required to live in close-knit groups, and to work, pray, and meditate together. Buddhist monks are exhorted to cultivate "spiritual friendships" and give thanks for the religious community. Sufi dervishes consider the communal invocation of Allah's name an essential part of the path to God. In Roman Catholicism, the rule of St. Benedict, which has guided the Benedictine orders for sixteen centuries, is essentially a guide to living in groups. The monks of Worth Abbey in

West Sussex, England, go so far as to call themselves "experts in community living."[2]

The work of the writer is a precarious balance between the private universe within and the complicated world of bills and bosses, families and friends. Just as solitude offers a space to rest and grow, community enables writers to develop the deep empathy and respect required to create writing that is courageous and true. And, just as solitude must be cultivated and nurtured, writers need skill to realize the full gifts of communal life.

COMMUNITY AS INSPIRATION

Solitude may give us the freedom to write, but what we write *about* comes from other people. The interactions that make up our lives as members of families, workplaces, countries, and the world community are the raw materials from which we create. What would we write about if we didn't know what it was to love a grouchy uncle, play with a three-year-old, or flirt with a stranger on the bus?

All writers derive inspiration from human interaction, but most miss opportunities to fully exploit that fertile source of material. Reworking some of our basic ways of relating to family, friends, and coworkers—even those we dislike and wish to avoid—and practicing new ways to think about our roles in our various communities can open up the richness of human relationships, offering us vast reserves of material to create from.

Magic Beans

Anyone who has lived in a family knows that even the most loving of relationships entails considerable amounts of conflict. Living rooms, classrooms, workplaces, and public spaces are often sites of intense discord. Conflict sometimes stems from a lack of love, respect, or communication skills, but it more often comes about simply because every individual comes into a relationship with her own needs, desires, and fears.

While disagreements are often miserable for the people going through them, for the writer they can be a lavish source of material. One of the epiphanies that writers come to when they use communal life as an inspiration is that the richest source of material comes not from harmony but from conflict. Stories and poems spring from tension: they may illuminate the comfortable and uplifting aspects of relationships, but it is friction that gives them life.

The key to turning discord into a story is the ability to discover its core. If we can get under the layers of confusion and miscommunication, we can find the hard seed at the middle of any disagreement. That seed can be thought of as a "magic bean," like the one planted by Jack of fairy-tale fame. Jack gave away his family's cow in exchange for a handful of what appeared to worthless beans. After his mother threw the beans out in a fit of rage, they grew overnight into an enormous stalk that led Jack into a land of giants and to many treasures.

Disagreement may appear so commonplace and worthless at first glance that all you want to do is throw it out—as Jack's mother did to the beans. But, like those beans, discord holds amazing potential, and planted properly, it can burst into astonishing growth:

1. *Pay attention.* The next time you are witness to or a part of a disagreement, pay close attention to what is said and done. If you are involved

in the dispute itself, you must be able to take a step back from it so that you aren't engulfed in emotion or focusing on how wrong everyone else seems. Don't try to ascertain other people's underlying motivations or hidden feelings. Focus on the network of interactions: how the participants communicate, who says what to whom.

2. *Write it down.* As soon as you can, write about the situation. At first, just create an outline of what happened. This outline should not involve an analysis of the conflict or an evaluation of who was right or wrong. Simply list what was said and done. The following short example is hypothetical but gives an idea of what to aim for in this outline:

   → David was making pizza.

   → Marcia said she didn't want pizza for dinner.

   → David said Marcia always complains about what he serves.

   → Marcia said that David should have remembered that she didn't like pizza.

   → David tossed a potholder down and stormed out of the room.

   Of course, most conflicts will be much more complex than this one, but most are no less banal. Try to record as much as you can, as closely as you remember it.

3. *Plant the beans.* Your first temptation might be to write a story about David and Marcia and their argument, but that is probably the least interesting or productive thing you can do. For one thing, you can't truly tell someone else's story: you don't fully know what is in their hearts. Furthermore, as long as you decide to stick with a script already prepared and neatly laid out, you ignore the magical aspect of the "beans." To unlock this magic, what you need to do is take this

basic conflict and create your own unique story from it. In other words, plant the beans in your own backyard.

4. *Add characters.* Start with two characters of your own. You can come up with new ones if you want, or pull some out of your earlier work. Plunk those characters down in the middle of this conflict. Instantly, the magic appears: as soon as different characters are faced with the situation, the conflict will take on new dimensions. Perhaps the couple fighting about pizza are Jake and Steve, life partners who have been together for ten years and are going through a rough patch. Maybe they are Dorothy and Patrick, an elderly couple, one of whom has serious health problems. Maybe one of the characters is abusive, the other meek; or maybe they're both master manipulators. Try the conflict out on whatever characters you wish. Where does it take them? How would these specific characters act it out?

5. *Heighten the tension.* Try ratcheting the conflict up a notch by intensifying the underlying issues. Steve might have his eye on another guy and gets angry quickly because he feels guilty about it. Perhaps Dorothy doesn't want pizza because she has been having stomach pain but doesn't want to say anything about it that would worry Patrick.

6. *Add new elements.* In the middle of the argument, the oven catches on fire, the couple's daughter comes into the room and begs them to stop fighting, or Steve drops a knife and it sticks in his foot. Try out a variety of ideas. Be as outrageous, subtle, or realistic as you wish. Fully explore what happens when you add even a single new element to your story.

7. *Experiment.* To further explore the creative potential in these magic beans, try another pair of characters or add different elements. Each

time, allow the story to go where it will. Let it take you along on the ride.

This exercise teaches you how to spark your creativity from the mundane events of everyday life. It helps you explore the ways people create and express emotions, and it offers a wealth of story ideas. But it has deeper benefits as well. By mindfully observing commonplace interactions among people and exploring the potential in each action and word, you become more keenly attuned to life's opportunities for learning and growth. Beginning with a simple interaction, expanding upon it in all directions, and delving deeply into its significance allows you to witness the endless possibilities of everyday life. As you discover the complex histories, mingled emotions, and hidden needs that underlie even the most ordinary of relationships, you become conscious of the depth and subtlety of human life, and the far-reaching consequences of even seemingly insignificant actions. That is the beans' real magic.

WRITING THROUGH DIFFICULT RELATIONSHIPS

A Japanese Buddhist monk at the Eiheiji Monastery in Japan admitted once that he chose a monastic life because he didn't care much for people. The monastery, he thought, would offer an escape from the annoying presence of others with their foibles and bad habits. Unfortunately, he soon learned that many of the monks he would be living, working, and meditating with irritated him as badly as the people he'd tried to get away from in the world outside. He was so distressed at the behavior of some of his fellow travelers on the monastic path that, at one point, he considered abandoning the monastery. "That was when I made a startling realization, " he explained. "I suddenly saw that the main thing I would learn at Eiheiji was compassion and patience. That was my great spiritual challenge."[3]

Most of us have never thought of entering a monastery—but we've all wished at some time in our lives that we had an escape from other people. Getting along with others is one of life's greatest difficulties.

Writing provides many ways of working through the problems of communal life. It can help us find solutions to conflicts, understand the needs of others, and communicate our own desires. It can offer us comfort when our relationships are causing us pain and provide an outlet for pent-up feelings. But perhaps its greatest benefit is that it can help us accept people for who they are. This exercise is aimed at fostering that kind of openness.

───────────────{ SACRED TOOL }───────────────

Radical Acceptance of Others

If writers are truly the voice of the human experience, then, like monks, we must be open to all of its manifestations. This *radical acceptance* is an openness to all people regardless of their behavior, attitudes, and beliefs. Radical acceptance is not easy. No one, except perhaps a few truly saintly people, can practice it all the time. But cultivating radical acceptance can open you to the great variety of human experience and allow you to observe, participate in, and write about the world without the encumbrance of anger and disapproval.

This exercise entails a series of steps by which we can write ourselves to acceptance. It takes time and thought, but the benefits it yields are worth it:

1. *Write your feelings.* The first step is to express your feelings about the person you are having problems with and his actions in a writing meditation. Take as much time as you need to let your feelings out. Let them spill onto the page in all their grotesquerie. Allow yourself to feel upset as you write and don't hold back.

2. *Identify key elements.* When you have finished, take a break—a whole day if you like, but at least ten minutes—then come back and read your meditation. As you do, underline phrases that seem particularly significant. Paying special attention to those phrases, look for patterns in what you've written. You may find that your feelings were not what you thought they were. Perhaps you're not as angry as you thought or you're just using anger to cover up hurt or jealousy. You may discover surprising levels of emotion. But it is also perfectly all right if you find that you have simply reiterated what you knew you were feeling already.

3. *Create an inventory of your feelings.* Working from your writing meditation, identify and name your emotions. On a separate sheet of paper, write each emotion out as a single sentence: "I feel angry." "I feel deeply sad." "I am full of rage." Try to include all the different feelings you have. Don't editorialize or explain; just state your emotions in the plainest words possible—but after each statement, leave space for more. Take care with this part of the exercise because the rest involves building on these statements step by step.

4. *Look for causes.* When you have concluded your feeling statements, add to them by stating the causes of your emotions. At the end of each statement, write the reason behind it, such as, "I am angry *because my neighbor filed a complaint about my dog*" or "I feel hurt *because my father is often distant toward me.*" Keep a couple things in mind as you do this part of the exercise:

    ✦ Try to keep your statement down to a single sentence. You don't want to delve deeply into your feelings right now: that usually just gets us tangled in emotions and judgments, which isn't what we're after here.

→ Make sure to write with the clarity that comes from distance. Write, "I am angry because my son has gotten arrested for defacing public property" not "I am angry because my ungrateful, immature son has disappointed me again."

Your statements should end up something like these:

→ I am angry because my son has gotten arrested for defacing public property.

→ I am enormously frustrated because he promised not to get in trouble again.

→ I am embarrassed because the neighbors will know about it.

→ I feel guilty because I think I must have done something wrong for him to be like this.

→ I am worried that he might ruin his future.

5. *Identify your wishes*. Expand on your feeling statements even more, by stating what you *wish* were true. The parent writing about his frustration over his son might add:

→ I wish he were more responsible.

→ I wish I knew what to do to change his behavior.

→ I wish he'd get in with another crowd.

6. *Do a reality check*. Now for the final addition to our feeling statement. This time you are going to add a reality check. You are going to remind yourself that wishes are wishes, not truths, and not all of them can be realized. In these statements, we do not negate our wishes, nor do we pretend that the behavior of the other person is all right. Instead, we affirm what we wish even as we go on to remind ourselves that this particular wish is not, at this time, true. In the end, your statements will look something like these:

- → I wish I knew what to do to change my son's behavior, but I accept that I don't know and that parents can't always control their teenagers' actions.

- → I wish he'd get in with another crowd, but I accept the fact that kids his age pick their own friends, and they don't rely on parents' opinions when they do.

It is important to realize that this kind of radical acceptance does not mean you approve of the actions that are upsetting you. You are not saying that it is perfectly all right for your son to get into trouble. Never think that it is acceptable for someone to harm you. This exercise also doesn't mean you shouldn't try to repair the situation, if you can. What you are saying is that the event happened and that you accept that it happened. You can't go back in time and make it not happen, and you can't always control the other person— even if he's your child. It is a way of realizing that much of life is simply out of our hands and that the best way to work toward a solution is to be open to the fact that there are many things we can't control.

Practicing radical acceptance doesn't hinder our ability to confront the things that are harming us. Rather, it brings the clarity we need to act effectively. It shines a light on the situation so that we can identify the true nature of our feelings and their source. And it eases our pain by helping us realize that the world cannot always be the way we wish.

For writers, radical acceptance is essential. It helps us expand the scope of our writing by keeping us open to a wide variety of ideas and by allowing us to view even activities we disapprove of with a clear eye. By helping us see beyond our own perspectives to the motivations and feelings of other people, radical acceptance enables us to create deeper, more insightful work.

SELF-AWARENESS IN COMMUNITY

Perhaps the greatest blessing of community is that it offers us a view of ourselves that we do not have access to in solitude. Community acts like a multidimensional mirror reflecting back to us our way of being in the world. In community, we can discover what makes us feel safe, what makes us fearful, and what sends us into a snit, a reverie, or a crying jag. When we pay attention, we can see the patterns of our behavior and the feelings underlying them, and we can evaluate whether they operate for the good or the bad.

For the writer, this awareness is a double blessing. It offers glimpses into ourselves that are indispensable for both the spiritual path and for writing. What we recoil from in life is often what we evade in our writing, and what we are drawn to in life shows up in our work even when we think we're avoiding it. If we are irresponsible, inauthentic, or dishonest with other people, our writing is likely to ring false as well—just as our generosity and caring will show through in everything we write. In this way, our lives in communities and our lives as writers interweave, reflecting and supporting each other.

-------------------------------{ SACRED TOOL }-------------------------------

Listening to Your Greek Chorus

In ancient Greek theater, the actors were accompanied onstage by a chorus. Nothing like the chorus lines of Broadway, the Greek chorus served as commentators and observers. They explained the action and gave background information. They clarified the themes of the play and showed the audience the hidden causes and impulses behind events. The chorus also served as a kind of consciousness for the characters. They offered essential insights and expressed things the characters could not, such as secret fears and desires.

The chorus was deeply interested in the fates of the characters and yet it stood apart from their victories and disappointments, unable to intervene in the affairs of humans. The members of the chorus wore identical (or very similar) masks to show that they didn't represent individual people and had no separate identities. They were, instead, states of mind or types of awareness.

The Greek chorus is believed to have developed from sacred rituals and symbols, and we can use the basic concept in our own spiritual work. Creating your personal Greek chorus can help you step back from emotional entanglements and write about your feelings and experiences with clarity and insight:

1. *Create your chorus.* Create a mask or a set of similar masks to represent your Greek chorus. Remember that your chorus contains no separate or individual personalities, so instead of trying to make the mask express a personality or mood, make it as neutral and expressionless—even mysterious—as possible. You may make the mask as simple or as intricate as you wish and with whatever materials work for you. A simple paper mask is fine, but some writers use clay or papier-mâché.

2. *Imbue your chorus with power.* In your imagination, endow your chorus with the ability to observe your behavior, know your thoughts, and offer you insights into your actions. Your chorus can express what you might be hiding—even to yourself. They can remind you of the basic themes of your life and let you know whether your actions are advancing those themes or hindering them. They can show you if your actions are benefiting or harming you and others. If you wish, create a ritual to imbue your chorus with these faculties.

3. *Invoke your chorus.* Whenever you have had a memorable encounter of some sort or when you are troubled about a relationship or simply when you want to reflect upon your actions and their impact on

other people, call on your Greek chorus. Imagine yourself beckoning to them. Visualize them entering the room—or the stage, if you like. Don't ask them questions or demand answers. Merely sit quietly and listen for their voices—or write and let them speak through you.

4. *Keep your chorus in perspective.* It is important to keep in mind that your Greek chorus is not there to nag, scold, criticize, or direct you. Its task is to witness, comprehend, and comment. One reason to give them identical masks is to get away from the trap of thinking of them as parents or teachers wagging their fingers at you. Also keep in mind that, although they might wail at your failures and exult at your successes, they don't get actively involved in your life and they have no power to change things. They can be thought of as both part of you and yet set apart: an element of your own consciousness that can step out of the scene and look down on it.

5. *Pay attention to your chorus.* Listen to what the chorus is telling you. Be patient and receptive, for they often speak softly. If they don't have much to say right now, don't give up on them. They may be silent for a reason. Perhaps you aren't ready to know the truth yet, or maybe other things need to fall into place before they can speak.

Over time, the chorus will gradually increase your awareness of the patterns in your behavior. As you see those patterns more and more clearly, ask yourself how they manifest not only in your interactions with others, but in your writing. Are you overreactive or quick to judge? Does that prevent you from fully exploring the complexities of your characters? Are you withdrawn, insecure, easily embarrassed, quick to anger? Look to see if those traits prevent you from writing with honesty and depth about difficult topics. All of the ways we behave in the world make their way to the page in one form or other: let your Greek chorus help you explore them.

6. *Put negative feelings to work.* Keep in mind that some of your emotions, even those that are generally thought to be detrimental, may actually be good for your writing. Writers can put grief and anger to good use in their work. In *The Courage to Write: How Writers Transcend Fear*, Ralph Keyes points out that the desire for revenge—which might seem to be an extremely destructive emotion—can actually be a powerful motivator for writers.[4] You certainly don't want to be writing from some tranquil, blissful state all the time. The important thing when you pay attention to your emotions isn't necessarily to overhaul your writing and your behavior, but to become aware of it, find its weak points, and deal with them.

THE WRITER'S RESPONSIBILITY TO COMMUNITY

Spiritual traditions throughout the world tell us that prayer and meditation are not enough: we also must act for good in the world. The scriptures of Sikhism tell us that "Heaven is not attained without good deeds,"[5] and the Bible exhorts us not just to listen to the word of God, but to become "doers of the word."[6] In Hinduism, good deeds are called *karma yoga*, which literally means *the path of union through action.*

Writers are not exempt from the requirement to do good. In fact, we have a special obligation because we have been given one of the most powerful vehicles for positive action: our writing. To truly use our work as a path to the sacred, we must be willing to employ it for the benefit of others.

Writing for the Voiceless

When you begin to look for them, you will be stunned at how many ways people can be silenced. Some simply have no access to modes of communication. For example, a researcher studying the welfare system in the United States found that media reports quoted sociologists, activists, and politicians—but almost never the people who were receiving welfare. The most important voices in the debate over social services were not being heard.

The voiceless may lack even the most basic means to articulate their needs as would be the case for young children and animals, neither of which even have the language to tell their stories. Often, the voiceless are simply beneath the radar of people's interests. Think of how many silenced people there are: refugees, homeless people, indigenous people whose cultures are disappearing, people with psychiatric disorders, people of the future, your own self as a child.

If you find this disheartening, remember that you have a powerful way of aiding the voiceless: you can write what they cannot say. Try these ways of serving as the voices of those who are silenced:

1. *Write about times you have felt silenced.* Empathy for voiceless people comes largely from our own experiences. Describe the way you were kept from speaking and delve into the feeling of being silenced. Write for that earlier you. Say what you wanted to say but couldn't when you were five or twelve or twenty-two—or just last week.

2. *Keep a journal.* Record times you witness someone being silenced. Note the ways their concerns are negated or trivialized. Explore in your journal the reasons they are silenced. Is it because they don't fit in? Is it because they threaten the mainstream in some way? Is it simply because they are a small group and easily overlooked?

3. *Serve as an advocate.* Write about silenced people. Pen letters to editors, opinion essays, informational articles, poetry, and fiction bringing the plight of the silenced to the attention of others. Donate your time and expertise as a writer to a nonprofit. Listen carefully to those who are silenced and dedicate yourself to acting as a conduit for what needs to be said.

4. *Take care in the role you play.* One pitfall you must watch out for is the tendency to speak *for* silenced people. Unless you are a member of the group itself, do not try to write as if you were one of them. No matter how good your intentions, putting words into their mouths is another form of silencing—and perhaps the most insidious.

5. *Avoid condescension.* Keep in mind that you are not some high and mighty person stooping to help the less fortunate, but someone who is benefiting deeply from their acquaintance. Do not approach this good work as if your are a knight in shining armor. Remember that those you write about are repaying you many times over: they are offering you their lives as ways to help you grow and as raw material from which to create stories.

COMMUNITY AS A GIFT TO THE WRITER

As writers we often feel that the many communities we live and labor in are major detractors from our work. The requirements of day-to-day community life eat up our time, steal our energy, and chip away at the stillness we need in order to write. Few writers have not at one time or another wished they could go off to live as a hermit—at least until their current novel is finished. What we often forget is that, for every minute we spend on it, community rewards us a thousandfold. It provides us with emotional support and boosts our strength for the hours we spend writing alone. It offers us ideas and insights. It keeps us centered and grounds our work.

It is easy to overlook the gifts community offers. Unfortunately, the more we ignore them, the less they benefit us. When we see our lives in community as a sinkhole for our time and energy rather than as a horn of plenty, chock full of gifts, we become blind to the blessings of community. We can't draw inspiration from something we see as an interference. As a result, it's important that we remind ourselves of the gifts of community and continually renew our appreciation for them.

<hr>

—————————————————{ SACRED TOOL }—————————————————

Expanding the Circle

If as writers we are to truly appreciate others, we must be open to human life in all its manifestations—and we must be willing to stretch beyond our small group of friends, relatives, and coworkers. This doesn't just mean branching out to meet more writers and others who share our interests and values, but going out into the world and interacting with people we would normally not know.

Be sure to set reasonable boundaries. Never befriend anyone who might pose a threat to your safety. Going to the limits for our art is all fine and good, but you'll be a much better writer alive and healthy—putting yourself in danger is not a heroic approach to writing, just a naïve one.

There are many ways to start interacting with other people:

1. *Go beyond your circle.* If you've had no experience with disabled people or immigrants, volunteer to work with them. If you are up for a more challenging experience, you might try volunteering at a homeless shelter, a battered-women's facility, an organization for troubled teens, or even a prison.

2. *Befriend people with different values.* Visit a church, synagogue, mosque, or temple whose practices are very different from your own. Get to know the people there. Become acquainted with those whose political views conflict with your own. Befriend people with less or more education, wealth, or status than the people you normally associate with.

3. *Consider who you don't know.* Think of the kinds of people you've never gotten to know well: babies, elders, people who are illiterate, people who are depressed, people with terminal illnesses. Seek them out.

4. *Keep a journal of your experiences.* Note the ways others react to you and your responses to them. Keep track of your feelings. Explore in writing the dimensions of the lives you are getting to know.

5. *Be aware of difficulty.* You should be aware ahead of time of how difficult this exercise may be. Interacting with others whose life experiences and core values are fundamentally different from our own can sometimes be deeply disturbing. Going in with that knowledge can help bolster you in the face of some unpleasant surprises.

6. *Go in with the right attitude.* The point of view you bring into this exercise is vitally important. Don't see yourself as an observer taking notes for your next novel or an artist who is above the people you write about. You must have a genuine interest in whomever you are getting to know, and be willing to open yourself to them sincerely and with love. For one thing, it is unethical to befriend people just for what they can offer you as a writer. For another, if you come to know people with that motivation, it will clearly show in your writing. It is not difficult to spot writing that comes out of a kind of superficial, detached observation rather than genuine empathy and concern.

7. *Review your journal.* After a few weeks, go back and read your early entries. Compare the reactions you had when you first started out to the way you feel now. You may be surprised by how your attitudes have changed.

Working with Archetypes

It is often difficult to understand the roles people play in our lives. Gaining a clear picture of how others have shaped our experiences in the world can deepen our appreciation for them—even for those who have hurt us. Clarifying how other people have contributed to our journey through life can make us aware of our debt to community and give us profound insight into our writing and ourselves.

An awareness of the effects people have on one another also has a direct effect on the quality of our writing. Understanding the complex roles people play in the lives of those around them helps us create more layered work that goes deep and rings true.

One way of shining light on the contributions of others is through the use of archetypes. In the fields of mythology, psychology, and literature, an *archetype* is a character who provides a model of common human experiences and responses. We are familiar with many of them from well-known fairy tales: the evil witch, the stalwart hero, the maiden locked in a tower. Archetypes express ways of being in the Universe by distilling complex personalities and relationships down to their essence. They are part of the collective unconscious shared by all humankind.

When we explore archetypes, we instinctually recognize ourselves and others in them. Although archetypes are often used to explore our own personalities, in this exercise, we are going to look not at the ones we find within ourselves, but at the archetypal roles other people play in our lives.

Before beginning this exercise, study the short descriptions below or read up on archetypes to get a clear sense of their characteristics. Archetypes can be divided into two general groups: allies and enemies. An ally is anyone who helps or supports us. In folklore, allies stick by the hero, offer her comfort, tell her the secret words that will open the castle gates, or give her the magic sword that will slay the demon. In real life, allies offer know-how or sound advice, a soft place to fall, encouragement, or anything else that moves us along on our journey. Some kinds of allies include:

→ *The mentor*: A person—usually older—who knows the ropes and helps you develop the skills you need for your journey. Teachers, professors, and bosses often serve as our mentors, but a mentor can also be the grandmother who encourages you to follow your dream or the friend who explains the best way to get an agent.

→ *The sage*: The folkloric hero often comes across a wise old man or woman who teaches him, protects him, and sometimes gives him gifts to help him along his way. Often, the sage appears just when the hero needs advice or help. In *Star Wars*, Yoda was a sage for Luke Skywalker. In real life, a sage need not be old, but she does need to be especially wise and willing to share her wisdom. A minister, therapist, spiritual guide, or simply a wise neighbor can act as a sage in our lives.

→ *The sidekick*: We see these comic characters in old westerns, but often fail to realize that others sometimes play this part for us. A sidekick is a friend whose main role is to provide you with laughter—such as the pal who is always lighthearted and can make you see humor in the worst of situations. But the sidekick offers more than comic relief. He also prevents us from taking ourselves too seriously, keeping us grounded when we get caught up in our own dramas.

→ *The angel*: Cinderella's fairy godmother is a perfect example of the angel archetype in folklore. In our lives, the angel is the person who always comes through, often with little thought of his own needs, and always with love. Whether he helps us search in the rain for our lost dog or drives us to work when our car is in the shop, the angel would never dream of accepting payment and is always sincere in his wish to help.

Enemy archetypes are those who wound, betray, or hinder you. An enemy isn't necessarily a villain. Anyone who has held you back, hurt you, led you astray, or interfered with your journey—even unintentionally—is an enemy. As with allies, enemies come in many guises:

→ *The nemesis*. This enemy isn't someone murderous or evil, but a rival who attacks you in minor ways. The coworker who belittles your work, the so-called "friend" who talks behind your back, the jealous sister who ridicules you to make herself feel less insecure. If we allow him to get to us, our nemesis can make our lives miserable, but if we see him for what he is—usually a weak, anxious person who is often trying to give himself an identity by becoming our opponent—then we can laugh him off.

→ *The threshold guardian*. This is a very specific kind of enemy— one who crops up to stop us whenever we approach a change in our life. In folklore, this is the gatekeeper who warns the hero not to enter the forbidden castle or someone who advises her to quit her quest and go home. You have undoubtedly come across threshold guardians in your own life. You are about to buy your first house when a friend calls to point out all the negative aspects of home ownership. You are thinking of returning to school, but your family tells you you're too old. Threshold guardians often mean well, but if we listen to them, we usually come to regret it.

→ *The seducer.* We all know one version of this character: the Don Juan, the femme fatale—the person who lures us into sexual pleasure, often at our expense. But a seducer can also be anyone who entices us to do something we'd be better off leaving alone. If you've ever been urged to break a promise or the law, cheat on your income tax or your lover, try a drug or tell a lie, or just skip class for a day, you've come across the seducer.

→ *The shadow.* This enemy is your archvillain, the person who you most fear, who might have the most power over you, if you are not careful. If there is anyone in your life who has done you genuine harm—or would like to—he is your shadow. One writer who had just been through drug rehabilitation wrote about his old crowd—who were all into drugs—as his shadow (they could also be considered seducers). Another depicted her violent ex-husband as a shadow in her poetry.

Although most archetypes fall into either the enemy or ally categories, there are a couple who can be both:

→ *The shapeshifter.* This devious character is anyone who seems to be one thing but turns out to be something else—the Big Bad Wolf disguised as Grandmother, for example. The shapeshifter can be someone you thought was good but who ends up hurting you, or someone you distrusted who turns out to be helpful and kind. Examples of shapeshifters are the best friend who stabs you in the back or the coworker who you thought disliked you but who covers for you when you've slipped up.

> → *The trickster.* This complicated character is a game player and jokester with a sharp wit. She may seem to be a lighthearted clown but she can sometimes be shrewd or cunning. Often the trickster's jokes are very insightful—and at times, they can be cruel. Like the shapeshifter, the trickster can be a friend or enemy—and sometimes moves from one category to the other.

Once you understand the differences among these various archetypes, begin this exercise by looking at your own life:

1. *Consider the people who make up your life community:* lovers and business partners, spouses and next-door neighbors, bosses and best friends—virtually anyone you come into contact with. As you do, step out of your personal evaluation of that person as nice, obnoxious, smart, or foolish, and think instead of the part the person has played in your own journey through life. If someone has helped you, how have they done so? Does their help fall into the angel category or are they more of a sage? Are they a mentor or a sidekick? Has anyone gotten you in trouble by leading you to do something wrong, even though you knew better? You've found a seducer. Is there anyone who constantly tries to get your goat and seems to be bent on trivial rivalry with you? You've met your nemesis. One person may contain elements of more than one category or play different roles at different times. Play with the archetypes and see what you come up with.

2. *Appreciate the mix.* One of the benefits of this exercise is that it helps you clarify and appreciate the roles people have played in your life—it can even make you grateful for some of the people who have

hindered or hurt you. This is because a balanced mix of archetypes is important in life, just as it is in the mythological hero's quest. No mythic character would be much of a hero if everyone he met along the way was friendly and helpful. The hero needs enemies as well as allies—both are essential to his journey. When we realize that we need our threshold guardians and seducers as well as our angels and mentors, we can be much more accepting of the people who play those parts in our lives. When you can look at someone and say to yourself, "I know you—you must be my nemesis" or "Hey, you're acting as a threshold guardian," you can still your anger and start appreciating everyone as a necessary part of your life's journey.

3. *Write about the people in your life.* Pick one or two of the people you've identified as playing specific archetypal roles in your life. As you write about them, continually keep in mind the archetypes they represent. You don't have to change them or refer to the archetype in your writing: by simply being aware of their archetypal role, you will sharpen and focus your writing.

4. *Write about a specific event in your life.* Another way to use archetypes in your writing is to write about an event in your life with the awareness of the various allies and enemies who played a part in it. One writer wrote a personal essay about a teaching job she'd been offered in another city and her crippling indecision about it. She had wanted the job badly, but once it was actually offered to her, she couldn't stop wondering if taking it wouldn't be a huge mistake. As she wrote, she recalled a close friend who kept bringing up possible problems with the job: it didn't pay enough, the city wasn't attractive, the schools weren't that good. When the writer realized that her friend was acting as a standard-issue threshold guardian, her essay became more sharply focused—and so did her decision making.

In *The Prophet*, Khalil Gibran wrote that without love, you will "laugh, but not all of your laughter, and weep, but not all of your tears."[7] The greatest gift of living with others is the opportunity to experience the richness of being human. Community brings us our sharpest pain and most exquisite joy. It allows us to truly know anger, tenderness, sexual desire, jealousy, kindness.

Remember to write with an awareness that others—not merely those who comfort and cherish, admire and respect us, but those who annoy, infuriate, and even hurt us—are a gift from the Universe. They are all part of the experience of being human, and all offer us the richness of their lives as material for our work. Without them, we cannot write fully—in fact, we cannot write at all. Writing with that knowledge in mind and with gratitude for the gifts of community helps keep us open to others, and to the stories they offer us.

The monastic elements of the writing life provide us with a firm foundation. When we have worked on these elements for some time, we can see a greater stability, richness, and self-assurance in our writing. With this sound underpinning, we can move on to our third path, that of the shaman—a path that will send us into the astonishing, frightening, and delightful realms of the subconscious.

PART III | *The Way of the Shaman*

In a wooden *ger* in the frozen landscape of Siberia, a shaman pounds on a small, cylindrical drum. Metal disks and animal-shaped figures dangle from his tunic, clanging together as he begins to dance. He calls out to supernatural beings, invisible to all but him, telling them that he is searching for the soul of a man who lies near death in a corner of the hut. The shaman dances until he collapses, exhausted—the sick man's soul safely back where it belongs.

A Carib shaman in Guyana inhales deeply on a tobacco pipe and blows the smoke upward in an offering to the gods. She announces that she is going on a journey to the realm of the dead to heal a sick child. She dances, calling for the spirits to join her. In a frenzy, she raises her arms and spins. When she nearly passes out, assistants jump up to support her, but she refuses to stop spinning until she discovers the reason for the child's illness and learns the proper way to treat her.

In a leaf hut in Malaysia, a Semang shaman and his assistant sing in a language unknown to human beings, in an attempt to heal a rift between rival families. The voices are theirs, but the words are believed to be coming from luminous spirits communicating to the world through the two men. The shaman holds a palm leaf that connects him to the celestial realms. He praises the spirits, and asks for their help in healing his tribe.[1]

Since the time of the first glimmerings of human consciousness, virtually every society on Earth has had members who travel between the mundane world and the spirit realm. These extraordinary people—known today under the catchall term *shaman*—cross barriers between life and death, concrete reality and shadowy myth. They enter states of consciousness inaccessible to others. Their goals are to gain healing knowledge and aid from the spirits on behalf of others who have come to them with physical or emotional ailments—sometimes for an entire community. They act as psychologists, priests, seers, and performance artists. Anthropologist Joan Halifax calls them "specialists in the human soul."[2]

Shamanism has been nearly obliterated in industrialized cultures, but the need for shamans has not disappeared. In fact, in a world where rationalism rules, we desperately need people to serve as our emissaries to the mythological realm. In the West, this task falls largely to writers.

Like shamans, writers have a special connection with the world. They view reality through the lenses of imagination, intuition, dream, and myth—the very act of writing is the conjuring of a waking dream—and they are in touch with forces that can elude others. "Writing is similar to magic," says Sheila Gordon, author of *Waiting for the Rain* and other novels. "One never knows exactly how it's done."[3] Novelist Tim O'Brien describes the writing life in terms of "incantations" and the "magic dust" of language: "A writer is someone entranced by the power of language to create a magic show of the imagination, to make the dead sit up and talk, to shine light into the darkness of the great human mysteries."[4]

To cultivate the shamanic aspects of the writer's craft is to explore strange new terrain. It can tap into your creative energies and enable you to access deeply buried aspects of memory and imagination. It can sharpen your awareness of your role as a "soul specialist," and it may take your writing into areas you never knew existed.

{7}

Darkness and Healing on the Writer's Path

THE MOST IMPORTANT QUALITY of the shaman is her ability to journey into the spirit realm and to return with the power and knowledge to heal herself and others. This quest into the unknown leads the shaman's spirit from the plane of everyday life to another level of existence. The shaman may experience a descent deep into subterranean worlds or a flight upward to celestial realms. She may envision mountains of ice, caves full of disembodied voices, rivers of blood. Frightening apparitions, monstrous beings, or the souls of the dead often appear, but so may beings of light. The shaman comes face to face with the spirit world and returns to the ordinary realm with healing knowledge to share.

If you have ever found yourself moving through an imaginary landscape full of people, places, and events that exist only in your mind—as any writer has—you know what it is to travel to another plane. Writing takes us "traveling into the depths of the self," as Herman Melville put it.[1] To be able to write at all, you must engage a kind of "out of body" experience. You need to enter a realm that is independent of time and place, separate from the earthly sphere where your body remains, typing or scribbling away. "I think that novelists go out into a space that is essentially a psychic space—a commonly held space," says Clive Barker, "and report back and say, 'That's what I saw.'"[2] Isabel Allende expresses a similar experience: "I feel that there's a dark space, and I go into that dark space where the story is," she says. "It's like going into another world."[3] Suspense writer James W. Hall talks of "going down into dark or mysterious or uncharted places in my memories and my consciousness. Then, having to wake up again to life, to claw my way back into ordered, reasonable, rational, everyday, responsible life."[4]

The process of writing is itself a journey much like that of the shaman's. It is a walk through strange landscapes, where you meet your personal demons and engage your own special magic, and from which you return to the ordinary world changed. You move through a realm of myth, memory, imagery, trope, and dream. When we speak of the writer's *shamanic journey*, we are referring to that expedition into imagination or into what can be called the *mythic realm*. Some writers may view it as actual soul travel into other dimensions. Most view it as a personal sojourn in the subconscious or as a mental state that draws on intuition and imagination, and disengages, for a time, rational thought and logic.

One thing shamans and writers share is the sometimes disturbing nature of their work. Although the shaman's journey brings power, knowledge, and healing, there is no question that it can be a dark voyage. As Eskimo shaman Igjugarjuk told Arctic explorer Knud Rasmussen, the only true wisdom "lives far from mankind, out in the great loneliness, and can be reached only through suffering."[5] Shamans encounter all manner of terrifying monsters and evil spirits as they travel. Even more terrible is the sense of personal dissolution they undergo—an "ego death" in which they may envision their bodies being dismembered, devoured, or rotting into nothingness.

What do monsters and devoured bodies have to do with the writer's work? Plenty: writers plumb the depths of society and of our own subconscious fears and desires. We tunnel through the dark caverns of personal and collective memory, and we explore our often perverse imaginations. The demons we meet are the fear, shame, anger, and grief that we carry inside, the fearful images that lurk in our dreams, the remembrances of loss, betrayal, and violation that remain half buried until we invite them to emerge. It is this dark aspect of writing that has led fantasy author Matt Haig to write: "low-level misery is the default setting for most writers."[6] Julie Baumgold, author of *The Diamond* and *Creatures of Habit*, goes so far as to write of "the unabating misery of the writing life, the need to lie, to get away, to hide among those, like lepers, who do not know."[7]

Of course, many writers would disagree with such bleak depictions. We can and do write with high spirits and a sense of fun—just as shamans sometimes travel in celestial regions full of light—and all of us spend most of our time in the less dramatic phases of writing, for example, working at the mundane task of revision. But virtually all writers face times when they touch on the frightening or sad—and those difficult times may even appear when they are writing humor or lighthearted fiction.

If this dark journey seems too daunting, take heart. There are many things you can do to keep the fear at bay and to make the writing experience one of triumph. The shaman's journey culminates with healing, not horror. The point is for the shaman to return to the everyday realm, stronger and wiser than when she left. The same is true of the writer.

The mythic journey that we undertake during the writing process is one of the most thrilling and challenging aspects of the writer's life. Whether that journey is defeating or fruitful, traumatizing or therapeutic depends largely on the writer's approach. A variety of techniques, drawing on the wisdom and experience of shamans, can help us make the shamanic aspects of the writing experience rich and fertile.

Preparing Yourself
for the Journey

A shaman never undertakes his journey without preparing himself, his tools, and the physical space in which he will work. He may fast, chant, dance, or meditate to stimulate his powers. He often dons special garments or masks. He makes sure his implements—rattles, drums, bells, and other ritual tools—are in proper spiritual and physical condition. The place where his physical body will remain while his spirit journeys will be cleansed, blessed, and properly arranged.

Writers, too, must prepare before setting off into mysterious realms. Although it might be tempting to simply plunge in without much forethought, that seldom works well. For one thing, we can find ourselves facing long-buried memories or horrific imaginings without the resources to cope with them, leaving us feeling shaken and wounded. Such lack of preparation can also be a surefire route to blockage or avoidance. If you find yourself hesitant, floundering, or stuck, it may be because you haven't readied yourself enough to confront your personal demons. As a result, you simply shut down. Courage is a fine thing, but launching into a project that will tap into deep wells of memory and imagination without proper preparation is just foolhardy—and it never results in good writing.

———————————————————{ SACRED TOOL }———————————————————

Taking Inventory

One of the most important things writers can do is to determine whether they are ready to face the painful memories or terrifying imaginings that may lie along the path. If you are writing from your own life experience, you need to think about whether the memories you're tapping are too fresh or raw.

This is a very personal decision. Some writers can work even at the height of grief; others must wait months or years before writing about painful events. You must know where you stand on this issue and back off if you find the pain is too great. The same is true if you are relying more on imagination than memory. The fears that lurk in our daydreams can be as terrifying as anything the real world throws at us because they arise from the darkest crannies of our subconscious minds. If you are not prepared to face them, the demons may "take over," and both you and your work will suffer.

Although there are no clear-cut ways to determine whether you are ready to take on a particular issue, there are several things you can do to clarify your feelings:

1. *Explore your motivation.* Get out a sheet of paper and write the answer to this question: why do you want to work with this issue? Be as clear and specific as possible about why you have chosen this particular subject matter at this particular time. Writing out your motivation can often clarify whether this really is the best time. It can also help you shed unrealistic expectations ("Once I write my grief out, it will never bother me again!").

2. *Create visual aids.* Many writers find that visual representation of their feelings helps them get a better grip on what they're going through. One way to do this is to create a chart of your feelings. Consider the mixture of emotions you are feeling and draw a pie chart, with slices for fear, anger, loss, dread, regret, and other feelings. Fill the slices in with colors. Or make a list of your feelings, and draw one or more stars next to each one, depending on how intense it is. Although this may sound hokey, it can give you some distance from your feelings and help you see them with more clarity. If you find your pie has one enormous wedge painted a sizzling red and labeled "Rage," or your list has fifteen huge black stars next to "Remorse," your feelings may

be too intense to work with right now. Regardless of whether your findings are this clear cut, translating your feelings into concrete, visual forms can usually give you insights into them that you may not get from merely thinking them through.

3. *Listen to your body.* Try this technique to identify the physical changes you undergo when you are working with an issue. Sit quietly with your emotions for a time. Don't judge them, try to force them to come up, or battle them down. Just feel them. Identify what is happening in your body. Does your stomach feel hollow? Are your eyes beginning to burn? Do you find that you're clenching your fists? These physical signs of emotion are normal and healthy: such reactions as sweaty palms or a tight feeling in the throat are to be expected when you're dealing with strong emotions. But an extreme physical reaction can be a sign that your feelings are still too raw. If your heart is racing, you feel lightheaded, a migraine is looming, you feel sick to your stomach, or you have some other severe change in your body, it is time to pull back. Your body is telling you something. Listen to it.

Remember that the goal of writing is not to become spirit-possessed, ravaged by the demons of your memories or imagination, but to use your shamanic power to master them.

———————————{ SACRED TOOL }———————————

Garnering Your Power

Once you are sure you are ready to face your demons, it is time to draw together your personal resources. It makes no sense to set off on these journeys without summoning your full strength. Going through a process of remembering and engaging your personal power will ensure that you have a triumphant and healing journey:

1. *Remember your power.* Before you begin your shamanic journey, write down a list of times you felt powerful and in control—for example, the time you called customer service and actually got them to do what you wanted, the day you found you could increase the weight of the dumbbells you use for your bicep curls, or the year you successfully quit smoking. Often, we simply forget that we have power. Creating a list of those times can remind us that we do. After you've made out your list, place it where you can easily glance at it when you write.

2. *Engage a feeling of power in your body.* Think of a time when you felt in command—use an item from your list, if you've made one. Sit with that memory for a while. Picture it in detail—the location, what you said or did, the other people involved, even what you were wearing. Allow yourself to feel that power. Identify where in your body you felt it. In your chest? Your abdomen? Your jaw? What physical sensations accompanied your experience of power?

3. *Move with power.* Before you begin writing, try standing and walking for a few minutes in a way that projects power. Begin with the physical memory evoked in the previous exercise, but this time, as you bring up those sensations, let them shape your posture and movement. Feel the command in your spine, neck, face, limbs. Allow yourself to literally stand tall. Walk through your house or around the block with a courageous stride.

Done before you begin your writing journey—and periodically along the path—these exercises will not only help you feel better when you confront your personal demons, they can help you deepen your writing. If we tiptoe into a cave as quivering wimps, we're not going to go far before deciding we've seen enough. If we stride in like the intrepid explorers that we are, we'll keep going and going, eager, despite the hazards, to see what is around the next corner.

<hr>

{ SACRED TOOL }

Creating a Lifesaver

Another way to prepare for the difficulties of the journey is to create something to grab on to when you're feeling threatened. The phrase "grab on to" can be taken literally here. Human beings have an instinct to literally reach out when in need. The first thing a person shocked by bad news will do is reach for a wall or a railing. When people are afraid, they physically grasp each other. Someone clutching a pillow as they weep is a familiar image. Finding something concrete to hold on to can help us keep going when the journey gets rough.

1. *Designate an object.* Choose some graspable object as your lifesaver. Use something solid and firm: a rock or piece of wood that fits in the palm of your hand is perfect, although some people find that something as small as a coin works. Some writers keep something on a chain around their necks, so the object rests near their heart where they can easily reach up and touch it.

2. *Endow the object with power.* It is important to establish in your mind ahead of time that the lifesaver has the ability to keep you safe. Imbue your object with the ability to protect and harbor you. Whether you need to merely think of your object as powerful or need to ritualize its status as a lifesaver, make sure that you know ahead of time that it is more than a mere stone or coin.

Designing a Safe Haven

Even with your personal power fully engaged and the security of a lifesaver, you may still find yourself threatened by the workings of your memory and imagination. To give us a greater sense of well-being as we journey, we can create a way to draw ourselves out of the troubling world we are writing about to a place of safety:

1. *Set up a retreat site.* Before you begin your journey, create a place you can retreat to when fear takes over. Make it a real place—the corner of a room, your garden, a favorite chair—not just an image in your mind. Don't choose the park a mile away or the beach you have to drive to. Your safe haven has to be easily and immediately reachable from the place you write.

2. *Make it safe.* The most important thing about a safe haven is that it must feel protected. The minute you enter that room or sit down on that lawn chair in the backyard, you must know that you are out of danger. It isn't relaxation, joy, or laughter we are trying to evoke here—although they may come—but a sense of safety. To make the place a shelter from the storm, put objects there that make you feel secure. If a picture of your spouse, dog, or favorite picnic spot evokes feelings of protection, put one in your safe haven. If the fragrance of cedar or cinnamon comforts you, have a scented candle or some essential oil there. If you remember your childhood as a time of security and nurturance, a favorite doll or stuffed toy might do the trick. Sound can also bring about feelings of protection. This might be a Tibetan singing bowl, a trickling desk fountain, or a favorite piece of calming music—but if a recording of the Three Chipmunks singing

"Alexander's Ragtime Band," makes you think of summer days with your family, by all means use it!

Letting Your Unconscious Be Your Guide

Shamans do not travel alone. Spirit guides and other benevolent beings join them on the journey. These helpful entities may seem to be bright, celestial beings or simple, kindly spirits. They may appear in the form of animals, humans, outlandish creatures, or disembodied voices. Whatever form they take, they offer guidance, comfort, and companionship along the path.

Writers, too, have their helping spirits. Strength, courage, humor, and confidence are some of those friendly companions. Another is the creative element within you—whatever it is that enables you to make poems or paragraphs out of sorrow and pain. Any of these can be envisioned as a benevolent being who leads you through the dark forests of your mind.

Creating or discovering spirit guides to accompany you on the journey can help you tap into your own strength and courage. The spirit guide is a personification of those forces inside you that enable you to face the murky depths of your subconscious and create from them. The guide can be invoked every time you sit down to write—or only when you find the going particularly rough. The guide may be nothing more than an image in your mind, but giving it physical form can add to its potency. Here are a few suggestions:

1. *Look for items to represent your guide.* One writer spied a tiny stuffed animal in the shape of an orangutan that seemed to be looking right at her from a bin in a drugstore. Something about the toy's expression gave her the impression that the animal knew her—was waiting just for her. She bought it, brought it home, and set it on her desk, where it has stayed for years. "I can't say it has actually given me

ideas for writing, but it always gives me comfort," she says. "When I feel my frustration build, I just look at its funny expression and feel lighter." Try keeping your eye out for an unusual figurine, picture, or doll that seems to "speak" to you. Instead of going to big toy stores, you might try rummage sales and thrift shops—places where you are likely to find an unusual item or one that has a long, interesting history.

2. *Write to your guide*. Try writing to your spirit guide. "I don't know how to solve this plot problem. Can you give me some suggestions?" or "I just don't have the energy to write this morning. Please give me a boost." Or you could try, simply, "Be with me on my journey today." Directly addressing your subconscious this way can yield surprising results.

3. *Construct a guide with your own hands*. If you enjoy handicrafts and find greater power in things created with your own hands, try constructing a spirit guide. Use whatever materials you wish—even a jumble of odds and ends pasted together. You may feel a special sense of connection to something you've made yourself that can be a special aid as you write.

4. *Develop your own ideas for a spirit guide*. A writer might imagine his guide to be a guardian angel, an elf, the garden gnome sitting on his neighbor's lawn, or the sock monkey he's had since he was six. Some think of their favorite authors as guardian spirits and keep pictures of them on their desks—Herman Melville imagined the great writers of the past holding out their hands to him.[8] Use your imagination to come up with your own ideas for a guide. Sometimes the best way to do this is to simply keep your mind and eyes open—just as in the shamanic journey, your guide may appear when you least expect it.

Preparing to Meet Your Demons

The actual challenges you will confront on your shamanic journey are the memories, fears, and pain that lie buried in your subconscious. Regardless of what you *plan* to encounter, once your start writing, you aren't really in charge and there's no telling what can come up. In fact, the exciting—and nerve-racking—aspect of the writing journey is that there's no predicting what will arise.

Nonetheless, we can stave off some of the trepidation we feel at meeting our demons by preparing for the encounter. Creating visual symbols for the "evil spirits" and ordeals in our lives can help us to remember we are on a journey into the mythic realm and to feel in control:

1. *Visualize your challenges.* If you are going to write about a painful experience or pen a fictional tale about something that makes you uneasy—both of which entail dredging up disturbing material from the subconscious—one way to garner strength is to visualize it as a physical challenge you confront on your journey. Perhaps the humiliation you felt in second grade will appear as a pack of ravenous ogres; maybe your loneliness after your divorce is a howling ghost blocking your way. The discomfort you feel as you write a poem or fictional story about a kidnapped child may be a river of ice you must cross or treacherous cliffs you must climb.

   You can also visualize the fears and insecurities you feel about your writing, the blocks that are holding you back, the lack of confidence that is keeping you from writing to your full potential. One writer borrows from an episode of the TV show *Northern Exposure* and imagines her low self-esteem as a mean little man who follows her all through her journey, needling her and pointing out her every flaw. Another envisions her anxieties about her writing skills as sharp scissors snipping at her heels. A writing block might be a boulder in your path or a slobbering, fat ogre blocking your way.

This kind of visualization makes our challenges feel concrete and manageable. "There it is: that gorge of fire I must cross," we say to ourselves or "Here's my loneliness in the form of a steaming swamp" or "The demons of shyness that tormented me in high school—here they are! I always knew they'd be ugly." Once we see them as actual *things* we must deal with rather than as amorphous phantoms with no substance to grab on to, our fears stop being quite so terrible.

2. *Visualize your power over the evil forces.* Once you have visualized the various barriers and beings you might face on your journey into the mythic realm, visualize the power you have to deal with them. Have a thousand-mile-high mountain of ice to scale? No problem: you possess the magic to lift yourself over it. Is a flesh-eating monster chasing you? Don't forget your shield of invisibility.

Preparing for the journey in this way can help us ready ourselves physically, emotionally, and mentally. Although you may be among the rare writers who go spiraling away into the realm of imagination the minute they sit down to write, and return to the here and now hours later feeling rested, most of us need this preparation to enable us to journey at all—and to help us make the journey a safe and productive one.

TRANSITIONING INTO THE JOURNEY

Even when he is fully prepared, the shaman isn't instantaneously beamed into the other realm. He eases into it, transitioning gradually through a series of stages, often over many hours. Writers can't usually take hours to get started, but we can't simply race off into the mythic realm either. Like shamans, we must be patient, take our time, and shift gradually into the realm of imagination.

Neither the shaman nor the writer can control how long it takes for the journey to begin. It can be a difficult process. But we can employ a variety of exercises to ease the transition into the mythic realm and to help us take the first steps across the threshold.

Setting the Stage through Ritual

Rituals are an essential part of most spiritual paths. They demarcate sacred spaces and times. They set our actions apart from the normal course of everyday life. They help us slow down and focus, to be mindful of what we are doing. In communal settings, they give participants a sense of belonging and unity. One very common use of ritual is to facilitate transition: rituals help us move from childhood to adulthood, from being a single person to being part of a marriage partnership, from life to death—and from the realm of everyday life to that of the spirits.

The practice of shamanism always entails ritual. The shaman may don special garments, recite certain words and phrases, perform precise bodily movements, or ritually cleanse the site. Sometimes she will eat or drink particular foods, take a ceremonial bath, or place the shamanic implements in a particular configuration. These actions are highly symbolic—and absolutely essential for the shamanic journey. They are used to formalize the shaman's respect for the work she is about to undertake, to strengthen her resolve, and to provide a transition from her day-to-day persona and her sacred shamanic role.

Writers, too, use rituals—and in ways very similar to the shaman's. Sitting down to write requires us to still our bodies and minds and shift our attention away from the activity going on around us. Setting up small rituals is an important way to segue into your writing, to honor your sacred work, and to bolster your courage. Just as ritual helps usher the shaman from the roles and expectations of the ordinary world to the spiritual realm, the writer, too, needs a transition between daily life and the sacred work of writing.

Ritual is highly individual, and it can take some trial and error to figure out what works best for you. Cynthia Leitich Smith, author of books for children and young adults, writes in her sunroom in the middle of the night with a cat on her lap and the lights off.[9] Truman Capote wrote only on a certain type of yellow paper—and always in bed.[10] Chilean novelist Isabel Allende even waits for a specific day of the year—January 8—to begin a new novel.[11] Here are some suggestions for developing your own rituals:

1. *Prepare your tools.* Many writers feel they have to organize their writing space and implements before they write. They may sharpen pencils, arrange their papers in a neat stack on the right-hand corner of their desk, and adjust the blinds just so. Although these actions may serve a practical purpose, the fact that they often entail predetermined and very specific kinds of actions testifies to their ritual nature. In fact, they are very similar to the cleansing rituals performed by shamans throughout the world.

2. *Eat and drink to prepare.* Many writers want to have a particular snack or beverage at hand. Perhaps you like to prepare a cup of tea and place it in a particular spot, even in a particular cup. Maybe a bowl of toasted almonds or, for that matter, marshmallows, has to be within reach. You may not have thought of those requirements as rituals before, but that is exactly what they are.

3. *Develop your ritual.* Some authors prefer more formal rituals, such as calling the four directions, smudging the area—a process of burning sage or other herbs in an area to purify it—or performing a blessing.

For others, the simple ringing of a bell or observing thirty seconds of silence is enough to set the stage for the work that will follow.

Try various techniques. Be creative. If something works for you, you'll know it immediately. If you're thinking, "I really want to start writing, but first I have to do this nonsense," you are definitely not doing the right ritual for you. If you are doing a ritual that suits you, it will feel natural and vital to your work. And you may find that it helps to prepare you for the deep, trance-like experience that lies ahead.

———————————{ SACRED TOOL }———————————

Grounding Yourself

Another important step as you transition into the world of imagination is to ground yourself in the here and now. Try resting for a moment before you write and then summon a clear notion of the day-to-day world, with its discomforts and trivial pleasures and all the things that tie us to it:

1. *Observe.* To get a strong sense of yourself on the physical plane, simply look around and take in what you see and hear. If you wish to spend time more firmly grounding yourself, you can write a description of the physical place where you are writing: "I am sitting in my bedroom and I see my green and blue comforter, the jacket I threw over the chair last night, and my favorite CD."

2. *Gather familiar items.* Another possibility is to collect a few of the objects that tie you to this world. One writer I know places her handbag next to her as a grounding device. Your cozy old sweater, your favorite mug, a photo, or whatever feels comfortably familiar will work fine.

3. *Think about where you are emotionally.* Are you feeling stressed by your office job or confined by an unsatisfying relationship? Perhaps you are content in your personal life and have a sense that you are "too happy" to write. Whatever is happening, keep in mind how your life is going and what is occupying your thoughts these days and include it in your narrative, map, or drawings. Clearly depicting where you are in ordinary time and space gives you a starting point on your writing journey, and a place to return to.

───────────────────{ SACRED TOOL }───────────────────

Invoking Trance

Trance or *ecstasy*—an altered state of consciousness unlike normal wakefulness or sleep—is essential to the shaman's voyage. It is the ecstatic state that enables him to leave this world: without it, he remains firmly in the here and now. In trance, the shaman's awareness is so finely tuned that things that are normally obscure become clear and comprehensible. In other ways, the shaman's consciousness is sharply limited: a shaman may be entirely unaware of the immediate physical surroundings, of what she is doing or saying in the ordinary world. This dropping away of the mundane world is the essence of the shaman's ability to enter the mythic realm.

Writers from Marcel Proust and William Wordsworth to John Barth and Gloria Naylor have talked about entering such altered states. Emily Brontë went into spells in which she felt that she had left her body and become a "chainless" soul, guided by visions.[12] Novelist Anne Rice refers to "surrendering to a trancelike state in which things make sense without analysis."[13] And poet Gwendolyn Brooks said a writer must enter a "self-cast trance" to create poetry.[14]

Unfortunately, this "altered state" cannot simply be engaged every time we sit down to write. Although some writers find it more easily than others, no one has complete control over when it will come. But, like shamans, writers have a variety of ways to open themselves to the "self-cast trance" and to prepare themselves so that when it does come, they are ready. For each of the techniques below, make sure to have your writing tools at hand to take up as soon as you need them:

1. *Drum your way into the trance state.* Drumming is an excellent avenue into the dreamlike state of the shamanic journey—and it is one that seems to work especially well for writers who are stuck or struggling with dry spells. The sound of the drum echoes the rhythm of our heartbeats and brings us to a primal place.

   You can either drum, yourself—various types of drums from around the world can be found in most cities or on the Internet—or you can listen to a recording. The drumming rhythm should be slow, simple, and not too loud. You should be in an environment that offers you privacy and in which you feel safe and comfortable.

2. *Dance into trance.* If you've ever danced for an extended period of time—or done any kind of highly energetic, rhythmic, physical exercise, especially to music—you know the effect it can have on your mind and emotions. Few activities are more effective in helping us enter a trancelike state. If you are so inclined, pull the shades and put on some music—whatever makes you want to move—and let yourself go. Dance as long as you wish to and then sit down to write.

3. *Experiment with skrying.* Modern Pagans use a divination technique called *skrying* that can help induce a trancelike state. Skrying involves gazing at an object or image for an extended period of time. Often, the best kind of object to use should be somewhat amorphous or ambiguous or something with a spiral or circular design. Reflections

in a pool or large bowl of water, a candle flame, swirls in a plate of sand, kaleidoscopic images, or incense smoke are ideal. The process is simple. Simply sit down in a quiet, private place where you won't be disturbed, set your object in front of you, and stare. Unlike many forms of meditation, skrying allows you to let your mind go wherever it wishes. Keep gazing and set your thoughts free. When you feel ready, start writing.

These techniques work especially well for people who feel stuck or blocked. They entail a kind of release or letting go that can open channels of energy and dislodge obstacles. Try them when you feel drained of creativity and see if the floodgates open.

{ SACRED TOOL }

Finding the Portal

All shamanic journeys involve an opening into the spirit realm—an entryway between this world and the other. Sometimes writers, too, find that creating a "portal" can help our transition into the world of imagination:

1. *Visualize a door, gate, or threshold.* Create a meditative state through relaxation and deep breathing to aid you in your visualization. Picture yourself as you are right now, sitting at your desk or table. Then picture yourself getting up and going to your portal. Allow an image of the portal to come to you. Perhaps you discover a strange cave in the mountains or take a fork in a road. You might even discover a mysterious door in your own house that you never saw before. Perhaps you need a special key to open the door, or a secret password. One writer imagines the mouth of a cave; another says "Open sesame," like Ali Baba in the ancient story.

2. *Create a depiction of your portal.* If you would like something more concrete, you can make a physical depiction of your portal in paint, pencil, clay, or whatever medium you like. Place the representation in front of you as you prepare to write. Another possibility is to use an actual door or spot in your house that you endow with the power to act as your portal to the other realm. One writer places a ribbon on the floor of her office, imagining that to enter her portal, she must step over the ribbon. "It's simple, but stepping over that ribbon gives me the feeling of moving from one state to another," she says. "I feel like I'm actually changing myself in some indefinable way as I take that step." Another writer uses a broomstick for the same purpose—engaging a powerful image from European folklore.

3. *Rest with your portal until it opens.* Whether you use visualization or a physical depiction of your portal, spend some time focusing on it. Pay attention to its details. Wait patiently for it to open.

Finally, imagine your patience rewarded: the ancient stone door creaks open, the drawbridge is lowered, the boulder magically rolls away from the mouth of the cave. However you visualize your portal to the mythic realm, see it as inviting you to adventure.

THE JOURNEY

By this point, you have equipped yourself emotionally and mentally. You have engaged your courage and confidence. You have prepared yourself through ritual or drumming. You may have a spirit guide, a lifesaver, or a safe haven. You have taken the steps to transition into the mythic realm. Now, it is time to begin your shamanic journey into that realm. Put your pen to the page or your fingers to the keyboard and write.

The writer's shamanic journey is an enigmatic thing. You can prepare for it, receive it, learn from it, and emerge from it, but the journey itself can only be experienced. Nonetheless, a few tips can help you as you write your way into the other world.

Surrendering to the Experience

The journey into imagination cannot be forced. You can't *make* it happen; you can only *let* it happen. For you to experience the journey fully, you must remain open to it, even when it becomes challenging. Unless you are feeling truly threatened, try to maintain a feeling of acceptance to whatever emerges. If you have prepared well, that should not be difficult. A few steps taken along the way can help:

1. *Imagine your guide leading you.* If you have created a spirit guide, take a moment now and then, as you write, to let her lead you. Although the spirit guide can play many roles—including merely offering advice and encouragement—one way to fully immerse yourself in the journeying experience is to give her more power. Picture the guide taking your hand and leading you down whatever paths she chooses. You can even visualize her carrying you or blindfolding you, putting her in complete control. If this seems creepy, remember that your spirit guide is really you—the part of you that is intuitive, uninhibited, and free. Let that part take over.

2. *Be aware of resistance.* Although a bout of panic or a deep sense of threat might make us flee the shamanic journey—and if we are intensely uncomfortable, we should probably withdraw—it is more common for the journey to fail in more subtle ways. The most

insidious problems are subtle forms of resistance that emerge along the way. You may feel this resistance as a kind of hesitation that makes you pull back from a topic, an idea, a passage. It might crop up as a feeling of fatigue, a loss of focus, a sense of frustration—anything that prevents you from fully immersing yourself in the journey. You might feel it in your body, as stiffness, restlessness, general discomfort, even a minor pain: our minds can find myriad ways to distract us.

Remaining aware that these signs are often ways of avoiding the deepest, most mysterious parts of ourselves can help prevent them from throwing up roadblocks. When you feel one of these distractions coming up, remind yourself that they are merely ways of preventing yourself from going deeper. You can use your imagination here. One writer visualizes those forms of resistance as people she meets on the journey who *seem* like helpers—such as an ostensibly kind innkeeper beckoning her into the safety and warmth of a cozy room whose real work is to lull her away from her quest. Another recalls the *Wizard of Oz* scene in which Dorothy and her companions find themselves in a field of poppies and drop off to sleep just before reaching the Emerald City. It's so much easier to nap than to climb that mountain of ice!

3. *Remember your power and the protections you have created for yourself.* In the midst of the journey, it is sometimes easy to forget the resources you created in your preparatory exercises. Try not to lose sight of them. When grief or fear threaten to overwhelm you as you're writing, physically grasp your lifesaver and keep going. As you write, try to maintain the physical sensation of power. If you feel yourself begin to succumb to feelings of fear or victimization, pause for a moment and go back to the memory of power, draw up your physical feelings of strength, and begin writing again. Don't allow

your physical posture to slump down into a victim's slouch. Sit tall and invoke the power you accessed prior to the journey. Making use of these important resources can keep you on the journey when you might otherwise retreat.

If these do not work, remember your safe haven. Sure, you're stepping into swift-flowing waters—but you're right next to solid ground. Forge ahead through the fear or grief as well as you can—but when memory or imagination threaten to overwhelm you, know that you can leave the journey and retreat to your protected place. Although the safe haven is specifically designed to take you out of the journey when the going truly gets too tough, the very realization that it is always there for you can sometimes keep you on track. If you can say to yourself, "All right, what I'm writing right now is painful, but if it gets too bad, I know my safe haven is waiting," you can often find the strength to go forward. If it does not give you that strength, by all means go to your safe haven—and with no guilt, shame, or regret. Give yourself a pat on the back for getting as far into your fear or grief as you did, and affirm that next time you will go further—even if just by a baby step.

4. *Don't reject anything.* The shaman can't pick and choose which demon will appear or which challenge she will face. She also has no idea what lush landscapes she may come upon, what angels may speak to her. Similarly, you might start out planning to write a comic story about your high school reunion and find yourself going off on your relationship with your wife, or begin with a fictional story and end up with a true one. You might find surprising sweetness in a memory you thought was bitter or find in a pleasant scene, a drop of gall.

Whatever comes up, accept it. Don't censor yourself. Get rid of "should," such as "I *should* be writing a piece of dialogue here" or "I really *should* abridge this scene—it's way too long." You will have plenty of time later to go back and revise. The journeying part of the writing process isn't for editing—it's for exploration and discovery. Facing the unexpected is part of the adventure. Keep open to whatever arises.

5. *Realize that the portal might be closed.* Some writers find themselves immediately transported to the other world and remain keenly focused on their writing and unaware of anything else for hours. But this doesn't happen often. More commonly, entry into the other realm is hit or miss. You may scribble away for a long while before you can enter the trancelike state. Or you may find the portal is closed to you this time and you will have to wait for another day to journey. The Sacred Tools provided here can make us open to the mythic realm, but keep in mind that the spirit world operates by its own cryptic rules. In fact, trying to force the portal open is usually counterproductive. Instead, accept the fact that the journey is not accessible right now. Explore the exercises you didn't do the first time around or repeat the ones you felt were the most useful. Plan to try again tomorrow or next week. Have faith: the journey will happen when it happens.

6. *Be grateful.* The writer's ability to travel into the otherworldly realms—whether you view it as an actual sojourn of the spirit or a metaphorical journey—is an extraordinary gift. It offers us views of the world inaccessible to others and it makes our work possible. Whatever happens, remember that you have been given a rare opportunity. Receive this precious gift with gratitude.

———•◦•———

When the portal into the mythic realm opens, you will find yourself in touch with a level of awareness most people don't even know exists. You will break through the straitjacket of logical thought to the world of imagination, where artistic expression becomes a manifestation of your deepest spirituality. In this place, your creativity will transform itself into something magic and unexpected, and your writing will soar.

{8}

Sacred Ground

AT A WRITING WORKSHOP she gave over twenty years ago, novelist and memoirist Maxine Hong Kingston pointed out something that held a strange, deep truth: "Stories grow out of the ground," she said, "which makes me wonder, when the ground is covered with concrete, where will our stories come from?"[1]

In these times of unprecedented environmental devastation, creating a strong connection with the natural world is not merely useful to the writer, but an artistic and moral necessity. And no one has a more rooted connection to the Earth than the shaman. Unlike "modern" people who tend to see the world in bits and pieces, each part judged mainly on its usefulness to humans, the shaman views the cosmos in its totality, as a unified whole. In the shamanic traditions, all existence is thrumming with life and energy, and all entities, both living and nonliving, are interrelated in a complex network of mutual cooperation. For the shaman, the sacred doesn't exist in some special building or far-off place, but is present on the Earth every moment, waiting to be witnessed.

Most shamans spend years learning about plants, animals, and natural forces such as winds and storms, and they are often required to live *in* nature for long periods of time. They may spend months and even years dwelling in isolated caves or sleeping on the bare earth. The shaman may study the life cycles of local plants and learn to converse with animals. The goal of this work is more than intellectual knowledge. It is an identification with the natural world, an awareness of our place as a part of nature. When that identification is complete, the shaman is believed to be able actually to invoke and meld with natural forces.

A connection with the Earth is also central to the writer's work. The natural world provides writers with a sense of meaning and connection, with inspiration, clarity, and balance. "We share bodies and minds throughout the organic world, right down to our genetic makeup," says poet Gary Snyder. "We are kin to the rest of nature."[2] Annie Dillard, author of *Pilgrim at Tinker Creek*, says that nature offers "mystery, newness, and a kind of exuberant, spendthrift energy," that it is an "impetus to the spirit."[3] More simply, poet Mary Oliver calls the natural world an "antidote to confusion."[4]

Shamans often serve as the voices of natural forces or of plant and animal spirits, "channeling" their messages to the human community. Writers sometimes report a similar connection with nature. David Guterson, for example, feels that the landscapes of his novels *Snow Falling on Cedars* and *East of the Mountains* use his voice to express themselves. "It's almost as if I'm compelled to sing these places," he says, ". . . almost as if they are insisting on it."[5]

Developing a deep, thorough relationship with the natural world can expand your awareness and ground your work. It can help you steer clear of intellectualizations and abstractions in your writing and keep your work authentic. When we come to realize that our stories grow out of the very earth, as Kingston said, we begin to see that our writing connects us not just to other people, but to all the beings that inhabit our world, and to the Earth itself.

Learning from the Wisdom of Nature

Shamans everywhere see natural processes as supreme organizing patterns. They live in awareness that nature has order and they operate from an unshakeable trust in the Earth, confident that the natural world knows the proper way to keep balance and health. And they're right: wherever humans haven't intruded, nature finds balance. The shaman has supreme respect for the wisdom of the Earth and is keenly attuned to its lessons. She spends years observing and experiencing nature not merely to learn *about* it, but to learn *from* it.

In modern culture, we have come to think of nature as rather inept and dangerous. For many years, we fought back "destructive" forest fires, unaware that they are a part of the natural cycle of a healthy forest. We build levees to prevent flooding, not realizing that many plants and animals have adapted to seasonal flooding. We drain swamps for farmland, wiping out entire ecosystems. We have trouble imagining that these natural processes have a purpose because we are blind to the wisdom of nature.

But writers must look beyond our society's blind spots and, like shamans, be willing to learn from the wisdom of the Earth. Seeking guidance from the natural world can offer us sources of connection, knowledge, and understanding unavailable anywhere else. "Come forth into the light of things," wrote William Wordsworth, "Let Nature be your teacher."[6]

Learning from the Earth

The simplest way to learn from nature is to simply let go of your preconceived notions and open yourself to its wisdom. Just being in a natural place and quietly observing can make you receptive to the wisdom it is offering:

1. *Select a site.* Bring your pen and notepad to a place where you can be alone in nature. Ideally, that might be a stand of redwood trees or a secluded beach, but keep in mind that there is nature in your own backyard, and if it is fairly quiet there, you don't need a more exotic setting.

2. *Wait.* Sit comfortably. Breathe deeply to shed the busyness and noise of the human world. Be quiet and still. For a while, just sit.

3. *Observe.* Once you feel grounded, look around you. Pay attention to your surroundings. Don't merely try to identify what you see ("This is a dandelion. That is a bumblebee."). Instead, give them your full attention. Take in shapes, textures, colors, light, shadow, and movement. Become aware of the sounds, scents, and textures. Smell the soil and leaves. Feel the crumbly earth and supple blades of grass, the hot sand of the desert, the chill of the snow. Remember that the odors of decay are as much a part of nature as the fragrance of flowers.

4. *Write.* As you do, ask yourself, "What is the Earth telling me? What can I learn? What lesson can I find in the ancient gray pebble, the busy working of termites, the wriggling worms, the tree bark and bird's nests and bees?" See what comes up.

Learning from the Weather

Most of us think of weather in terms of cancelled baseball games, powder-covered ski slopes, winter blues, and springtime romance. Of course, its effects are far more profound than altering our recreational plans and coloring our moods. Weather is tied to everything from the stock market to our food supplies, from our health to our architecture. In fact, all life on Earth depends on particular weather cycles and processes.

Unfortunately, our insulated, air-conditioned world has alienated us from the weather. It is easy to go through our days with little awareness of the profound and compelling weather phenomena occurring all around us. Experiencing and appreciating weather can help us develop a mindful awareness of our place on the Earth. Bringing that awareness of the world around us to our writing can add dimension and vibrancy to our work. There are a variety of ways we can do this:

1. *Write.* Find a place outside where you can write and do a writing meditation on the weather as you are experiencing it at a particular moment. Use all your senses, detailing the warm breeze on your face or the icy wind cutting through your heavy jacket, the rain spattering all about or the silence of the snow. Remember that weather has smells and even tastes as well as sights and sounds. Write about the way the weather makes you feel: Does the rain comfort you with its steady patter? Does the wind make you restless? Does the hot sun put you in the mood for a cold beer and barbecue? Write about how the weather is altering the visible landscape around you. Is the rain bringing out snails and earthworms? Is the cold turning the grass brown? Is the increased spring sunlight making lilacs bloom?

2. *Explore the gifts of weather.* Meditating on the sensory and emotional aspects of the weather is good—but it is only part of the story. To get in touch with the true significance of the weather, explore its gifts to the Earth. As you continue your writing, think about the effects of the weather on watersheds and wildlife, soil and air, the farmland that produces the food you eat, the forests that help clear the air of carbon dioxide. Depending on where you live, you might consider how a blanket of snow protects the roots of plants from freezing, how the lizards in your backyard use sunlight to warm their cold-blooded bodies, or how rain creates seasonal wetlands not far from your house that harbor entire ecosystems.

3. *Learn.* If you don't know much about the weather, ask and learn. Deepen your awareness of the weather by reading. Be like the shaman who learns about the forces of weather from elders—except that your elders have written books and Internet articles.

4. *Keep a weather journal.* Try writing about the day's weather every morning for five minutes. Do this for a few weeks—or even months. When you go back and read what you've written, you will find a record of nature's forces as they change through the seasons.

{ SACRED TOOL }

Learning from the Wisdom of Animals

According to the Wetsúwetén people of British Columbia, animals are members of societies and are as intelligent and aware as their human counterparts. The Koyukon people believe that animals communicate among themselves and understand human behavior and language. They honor animal spirits and even perform funerals for them not unlike human funerals. The Chewong people of Malaysia even have laws against ridiculing animals.

One of the great tragedies of modern life is our loss of respect for animals. We treat a few with love; the rest we have caged, trapped, killed, confined, and tortured. We may see some of them as cute or even fascinating, but we seldom believe we can actually learn from them.

Although most of the writers I know love animals, few of us take our affinity with them as seriously as many indigenous peoples. But a strong connection with the animal world can invigorate our writing. Recognizing our kinship with nonhuman animals and broadening our awareness of their intelligence and emotional lives can deepen our respect for animal life and make us realize how much these brethren can teach us:

1. *Choose an animal to observe.* The easiest choice would be one of the animals who share your home, but you can also observe a wild animal—a bird, squirrel, deer—who regularly comes into your yard or an animal at a wildlife sanctuary, making sure that the facility treats the animals ethically. The animal doesn't have to be a mammal or bird: a spider in her web or a colony of ants make excellent subjects.

2. *Observe the animal closely.* Have a notebook ready for unexpected details and your own thoughts. Watch the animal move, breathe, eat, defecate, and scratch. See how he interacts with humans and other animals. Pay attention to the times the animal stops to sniff at an object or swims to the surface of the water. Listen to the sounds he makes. If your cat is the focus of your observation, for example, you should take note of what catches her eye out the window, of how long she stares at it, and what she does in response to it. Trace her route through your house for at least one day. Careful observation

will show you patterns in her behavior that you may never have noticed before.

3. *Work through the monotony.* The biggest challenge in this exercise is that it can be excruciatingly boring at times. Many animals spend much of their day sleeping, sitting, and staring. Our contemporary brains, used to continual stimulation, often rebel against the need to wait quietly. The antidotes to this boredom are internal stillness and deep observation. Resign yourself to waiting. Keep observing when nothing is happening, when you think you should be doing something more important, and when your brain feels like it's about to implode. Learn the patience and quiet persistence the shaman develops in his long, arduous training. In fact, it is often just when you feel you have observed enough that the interesting stuff starts happening. Keep going a little while longer and see what comes up.

4. *Reread your notes.* When you are finished, let your notes rest for a day or two, and then look at them again. As you read, consider what you can learn from the animal. Then, with your notes as a guide, write about what the animal has taught you.

5. *Continue your observations.* If you wish to delve deeply into the animal's silent teaching, do this exercise for a little while every day for many days. Keep good records of the animal's behavior, of your reactions to it, and of what you can learn from it. The more you do this, the greater your understanding will be—and you may be astonished by what you learn.

ALIGNING SPIRIT AND LANDSCAPE

The writer's greatest strength, says Milkweed Editions publisher Emilie Buchwald, "lies in writing about a place they feel inside their bones."[7] According to essayist Barry Lopez, we each have an interior terrain that mirrors the physical landscapes we inhabit.[8] Buchwald and Lopez are speaking of more than simply having a connection with place. They are talking about bringing the quality of the land into our very selves, about melding physically and spiritually with place. Learning to feel a place in your bones can help you see that relationship between interior and exterior landscape and bring a deep relationship with place into your writing practice.

{ SACRED TOOL }

Becoming the Mountain

Practitioners of the Japanese religious sect known as Shūgendo speak of climbing a mountain in order to feel its presence inside of you. While most of us in the West climb mountains to get to the top, in Shūgendo the destination is less important than the awareness that you and the mountain are one. We can use a similar approach to increase our connection with any natural environment:

1. *Mindfully experience a natural place.* As with the other exercises in this chapter, a wild and remote setting would be ideal, but at least find a natural place away from cars and concrete. Walk through the landscape. Be aware of the nature all around you. See, hear, smell, and touch with awareness. After you have walked for a time, sit. Be still and feel your affinity with the natural things around you.

2. *Write your connection with the land.* Get out your writing materials. Begin a line with, "I am . . ." and complete it with one of the living or nonliving entities that is sharing your space right then. What are you? The dead log you're sitting on? The termites consuming it? The soil it is becoming? Pick whatever feels most real at that moment. After that first sentence, continue to write and see where it leads you. Once you have begun with something like, "I am the bark of this elderly oak tree," you may find your writing bringing you deeper and deeper into your connection with the natural world.

3. *Continue walking, waiting, and writing.* Some writers prefer to stay in one place and to write in more depth about a particular natural object or living thing. Others like to intersperse writing with walking. If you wish, walk again after you have finished writing. After a time, stop and do another writing meditation beginning with "I am . . ." (picking a new item this time). Repeat this process throughout your walk.

4. *Turn the land into a poem.* At the end of your walk, create a poem from your writing meditations. Use the sense impressions you've had. Write from the raw experience of the land.

Seeing the Interconnectedness of All Life

The Desana people of the northwestern Amazon believe each sound, taste, or aroma of the rainforest carries a message about their lives, the Earth, and the Universe. Their understanding of the world is just one expression of the universal truth that all of life is interconnected. The awareness of the interconnectedness of all things underlies all shamanic traditions. It is also a key to deep and rich writing, and there are a variety of ways to cultivate it.

Degrees of Separation

The phrase *six degrees of separation* has become popular in recent years. It refers to the idea that every person on Earth is separated from every other person on the planet by no more than six steps. The people you know personally are one degree of separation from you; the people they know are two degrees of separation from you, and so on. The idea has never been proven, and some people consider it to be an urban myth. But playing with the notion can yield interesting results—and can lead to an awareness of exactly how connected we all are:

1. *Imagine a person geographically and culturally distinct from you.* In this exercise, you will try to create a six-step separation between you and this real or imagined person. It is more effective if you pick a very unlikely person, such as someone living in a distant country you've never visited. You may use an actual or imagined person. She may be the unnamed woman in a refugee camp in Darfur whose picture you saw on the news, a Norwegian farmer you read about in an article about Scandinavian produce, or an inmate of a prison no farther than thirty miles from your house. If you can't think of anyone, one glance at a newspaper is enough to give you many possibilities.

2. *Envision your chain of connection.* Imagine that you are at one end of the chain of connection, and the person you have chosen is at the other. Your task in this exercise is to imagine the people who make up the chain. There should be five people between the two of you, which creates six steps from one end of the chain to the next. You may begin with people you really know, but very soon you will have to use your imagination to create possible links. At the end, you will

have something like this chain, completed by a woman in Detroit, linking herself to a spice vendor in Benares, India:

→ Me, a thirty-seven-year-old high school teacher in Detroit.

→ J. P., my best friend from college whom I still call once a month. She is a former pharmacist now going to law school.

→ S. A., the man J. P. used to date whose father had once been a missionary in New Delhi.

→ S. A.'s father, Rev. A., a missionary.

→ "Lakshmi Devi," the woman who cooked for Rev. A. in New Delhi.

→ "Kamala," Lakshmi Devi's sister who lives in Benares.

→ "Mohan Tilak," the merchant from whom Kamala purchases her spices for cooking.

In about the middle of this continuum, the writer switched from real to fictional people—she knew the identity of everyone through Rev. A., but filled in the connections from there to the spice merchant. Nonetheless, her chain of connection is convincing.

3. *Create a story or poem from the chain of connection.* Write a story or poem about the seven linked people in your chain. Write about the ways they are interrelated—or about how differently they live despite their interconnection. Play with the notions of connectedness and difference, inequity and balance. Consider other ways the same people might be linked—it is possible, if you use your imagination. Consider in your story or poem what these connections mean to you, to the others in your chain, and to the world.

This exercise provides a clear sense of how closely related we are, even to people living on the opposite side of the world. It shows that you could very well be related to a Mayan child or a miner in the frozen fields of Siberia by just six degrees of separation.

{ SACRED TOOL }

The History of a Meal

When a Cree hunter fells a doe, he believes the animal willingly sacrifices her life as sustenance for the tribe, and he handles her body with respect and gratitude. Indigenous peoples throughout the world have a deep connection with the animals and plants who supply them with food. Because many indigenous societies believe that all living beings possess spirits and great power, they cannot help but have a keen appreciation for them.

The shaman's relationship with food is tied to this awareness and gratitude. One shamanic role is to ensure that the community has enough to eat: shamans often undertake their journeys to help improve harvests and the success of hunters. Because of the power latent in food, the shamanic rituals sometimes entail consuming certain sacred fare. In some traditions, such as those of the Peruvian Amazon, the shaman adheres to a strict diet in which certain foods are forbidden and others obligatory. Many others exhort the shaman to show respect for food by treating it with care.

Every time we sit down to eat, we are utilizing gifts of nature, animals, and other human beings. Becoming aware of our debt to the many beings and forces that feed us gives us a fresh awareness of the interconnectedness of all life. Taking time to reflect on those gifts is an excellent way to deepen our connection with the Earth:

1. *Choose a meal to work with.* Any meal, ordinary or fancy, will work well—or you can work with just a single dish, if you want to do something a little less complicated.

2. *Plan the meal.* Give yourself a week or two to prepare for this exercise. During that time, write a list of the ingredients for each dish.

3. *Write about the ingredients.* For each item, write about the journey it has taken to get to your table. If you are planning a breakfast of an omelet with tomatoes and onions, a cup of coffee with cream, and an orange, you will have all the routes of those ingredients to trace. Begin with the eggs. Imagine the hen who created them with her body. Consider whether she lived in agony her entire life in a cramped cage—or more humanely on a family farm. Imagine where she laid the product of her body. Picture the person who collected the eggs. What was his life like? What did he think of the work he did? Consider the journey the eggs took—how they were transported, sized and packaged, and shipped again to your supermarket. Think of the person who unloaded them from the truck and the person who put them on the shelves. It takes time to do this thoughtfully for each ingredient, which is the reason for doing it well ahead of time.

4. *Prepare and consume the meal.* When the day comes, prepare the meal mindfully. Think about each ingredient as you add it. Consider the fuel it takes to cook the meal and the utensils required to prepare it. Eat the meal slowly. Fully enjoy your food and eat with gratitude to the human and animal labor that brought it to your plate, and to the Earth that provided you with all the ingredients.

5. *Write.* When you have finished, do a writing meditation on the experience of preparing and eating the meal. You will find that eating with gratitude and awareness has greatly heightened your enjoyment of the food you consume. It also serves as a reminder of our place in nature and our connectedness with all things on Earth.

THE LIVING PAST

To the Diné, or Navajo, the most important time was the past, when the foundations of the world were laid, and ancestral memory is the most valuable of resources. The Heiltsuk people of the Pacific Coast perform ceremonial dances to re-create the origin of the world and honor their ancestors, and Australian peoples speak of the Dream Time from which the Earth and all of its life-forms originated. Shamanic knowledge comes from traditions that go back thousands of years. Virtually all shamans honor their ancestors, the great shamans who have gone before them, and the histories of their tribes or communities. Part of shamanic training is designed to instill in the shaman a profound understanding of her debt to the past.

The great veneration for the past shown by indigenous peoples throughout the world stands in stark contrast to our own culture in which almost nothing is worse than being out of date. "You're history," says the TV cop to the captured felon. "That's all ancient history," we say to dismiss something that happened the day before yesterday. In our race for "progress," being "old fashioned" is nearly a crime. This lack of reverence for the past is reflected throughout our culture in our love for new things, our craving for change, our dismissal of elderly people, and our disdain for tradition.

This is a serious and generally overlooked problem for writers. Just like the shaman, writers work from traditions that go back millennia, to the times of the first tellers of tales: we stand on the shoulders of those storytellers. Yet, unlike the shaman, we almost never think about our literary "ancestors" or the role of the past in our writing. Furthermore, the writer's work grows from memory and history—even a futuristic story is an extrapolation from the past. Without an awareness of the past as an essential part of the present, the writer's work pales. When we learn to honor the past, we soon realize it is not just a boon to our craft, but a necessity.

Writing Your Family History Backward

Unless you're royalty, you may know little about your family before your grandparents or great-grandparents. This exercise doesn't involve hiring a genealogist to discover your family history, but transitions from real to imagined history, much as the traditions of indigenous peoples move seamlessly from history to myth:

1. *Write about your family history.* Beginning with yourself and working back in time, write a brief paragraph about each person in your family. Follow one line—such as only the women (mother, mother's mother, and so on), only the males (father, father's father, and so on), or switching gender from one generation to the next. If you don't limit your exploration in this way, you won't get beyond your sixteen great-great-grandparents.

   The further back you go, the less you will know about your forebears. You may be able to write only, "Great-Grandmother Elsie—born in Louisiana, daughter of a milliner." That is all right. We can flesh things out later.

2. *Merge into imagined history.* When you get to the point where you don't know about your ancestors, imagine who they might have been. Make up your great-great-grandfather's name, where he was from, and some of the most important elements of his life. Then go on to *his* father or mother. Pay close attention to the era in which each character lived. If the ancestor you are creating lived in the United States during the Civil War, don't forget the impact that conflict would have had on her life. If they lived in Japan during the heyday of the samurai, remember that in your depiction. You may go as far back in time as you wish.

3. *Draw a timeline.* If you wish, draw a timeline marking the lives of these real and imagined ancestors, or create some other visual representation of their connection with each other and with you.

4. *Write.* Now pick two or three of your ancestors (real or imagined) and write a story or poem about each of them. Or write about your lineage as a whole and the complex of events that came together to bring you to life in this place at this time.

One thing that this exercise does is make you aware of how close the past is. If you were born in 1970 and calculate approximately three generations per century, you only need to go back seven generations to reach the American Revolution, twelve to reach the Incan Empire, and seventy to reach ancient Egypt. We tend to think of previous decades and centuries as far away and long dead. Realizing how close we are to those previous times and the repercussions they still have on our lives today can dramatically alter our perceptions of the past. It can help us realize the interconnections between past and present and, most importantly, it can foster in us some of the shaman's reverence for those who have gone before.

{ SACRED TOOL }

The History of One Square Yard

In school, we learn the histories of nations. At home, we may learn a bit about the history of our families. But perhaps because we are so mobile in this era, we have lost our sense of history with respect to the smaller places that we occupy—the streets, houses, and patches of ground. While people of the past could tell you much about the history of their village or tribe, many of us today know almost nothing about the history of the cities we live in, let alone the city blocks. We can remedy this by engaging our imaginations to create a history of the place where we are sitting or standing right now—not the nation or state, but the one square yard we are occupying this minute:

1. *Do a writing meditation on a specific place.* Consider the spot you are sitting in right now—or a place you occupy often, such as the spot at your desk or your place at the kitchen table. This doesn't mean the city or community, but the one square yard you're inhabiting. Begin a writing meditation about it.

2. *Imagine the place in the past.* Write about what the place was like a year ago, five years ago, ten. Let your imagination keep going back through the decades. Think of the people who stood in this spot. Who might they have been? What might they have been doing? Go back farther until the building you are in disappears. What was in this place before? Continue going back and back, picturing the very spot you occupy at this minute. What was there a century ago, a thousand years ago? What was there when the first humans were walking out of Africa? What creatures walked (or swam) there in the time of the dinosaurs? Go back to the beginning of the Earth, when the place first formed—the same exact spot where you are sitting now.

3. *Read it back.* As you continue to sit in your spot, read back what you have written. Be mindful of the continuous stream of the past that stretches out behind you into time.

———————{ SACRED TOOL }———————

The History of an Object

Another type of history you can do focuses on an object. It works best with an object that we are particularly fond of, or that we use every day:

1. *Pick a common object.* Perhaps you want to consider the sweater you have on right now or the coffee mug you use each morning. Have the item in front of you or, if it is an item of clothing, wear it.

2. *Write about the way it is now.* Begin this writing meditation with the present state of the object: how it looks and feels, how you use it. Write about the feelings you have for the object. If you have particular memories of the object, include them. For a clothing item, you can run through places you've worn it, times you've washed it, dried it, spilled maple syrup on it.

3. *Follow the item back in time.* Imagine it going back to the store where you bought it. Who tried it on or looked at it before you did? Who put in on the shelf? Who took it out of its original box? If you bought the item from a thrift store, think of the people who may have owned it in the past. Travel back to the factory where it was made (or the several factories that assembled different parts of it). Imagine it separated into its parts—the yarn, dye, buttons, or whatever the item is composed of. Follow those parts back to the farms and factories where they were produced. Think of the labor—both animal and human—that went into producing those substances.

   Even though these histories are largely imagined, they still bring us in touch with the past. They make us aware that all of the things around us have histories—often long, complex, and interesting. Exploring those histories makes us realize what the Diné and the

Heiltsuk already know: we and everything around us are part of the same story that stretches back through time to the beginning of the Universe.

Claiming the Power of Nature

Linguist Andrew Goatley, who researched the way we communicate about nature, discovered that we almost always refer to it as either a powerless tool used by humans or an untamed threat to them.[9] This is a far cry from many other cultures in which the power of nature is acknowledged as a wonderful gift. Claiming this power is an important step toward deepening our connection with the Earth.

————————————{ SACRED TOOL }————————————

Becoming Animal

Earlier, we talked about an exercise in which we observe an animal with great attention and focus. That exercise is designed to help us learn from animals, to allow them to be our teachers.

This exercise takes us in a different direction. Instead of exploring what we can learn from animals, we will attempt to take into ourselves some of the great spiritual energy of our nonhuman kin. To do this, we transform ourselves *into* animals, get a glimpse of how they experience the world, and soak up some of their spirit.

The title of this exercise is a bit misleading: human beings already are animals. But becoming fully conscious of our animal nature and identifying with the lives of nonhumans is a way to increase our awareness that animals share the Earth with us, that they are made of the same fiber as we are, that they are our kin. Writing from the viewpoint of an animal puts us in touch with minds that are starkly different from our own—an excellent way of growing our creativity and intensifying the kind of understanding we can call *writers' empathy*:

1. *Envision an animal.* Begin by imagining an animal coming toward you. Certain animals come up frequently in this exercise—bears, wolves, and eagles are perhaps the favorites—but keep in mind that you can become any kind of animal. A dragonfly, a snake, a mole, a jellyfish—all offer rich opportunities for imaginatively experiencing our kinship with nonhuman animals. Observe carefully as the animal approaches. See his color, shape, movement. Hear the sound of breathing, paw steps, the beat of wings. See the animal stopping in front of you. Touch and smell the animal. Feel his fur or scales or feathers. Touch his beak, feet, fins, or tail. Breathe his scent deeply.

2. *Become the animal.* Now feel yourself becoming that animal, your body transforming. If your animal is a lizard, for example, feel your legs shrink and your toes lengthen. Your coccyx stretches into a tail. Your outer ears retreat inside your head. Your lower eyelids swell and the upper ones retreat. Your tongue elongates and flattens, and you feel scales sprout on your skin.

3. *Explore the world in your animal form.* Now you *are* a lizard. What does it feel like to walk with these four legs, to climb vertically up the trunk of a tree, to see with these new eyes? What does the Earth feel like beneath your feet? What does the world around you look like? What do you smell, taste, and hear with your new senses? What do you feel? Are you frightened of the humans around you? Are you keeping one eye overhead, searching the sky for predators? Do you sense the primeval urge to eat, find shelter, warm yourself in the sun?

4. *Write*. With your imagination fully engaged, write from the animal's viewpoint. Avoid cuteness and clichés ("I sure enjoy tipping my head up and howling at that round white disk in the sky!"). Focus on sensory experience and physical needs, on the way you imagine the animal truly experiences the world. If your imagination flags, go back to the body awareness of that animal and keep writing.

This exercise is an excellent way to stretch and activate our creativity muscles, but it also expands our consciousness and, most importantly, deepens our empathy with the nonhuman world.

{ SACRED TOOL }

Writing the Whirlwind

In one of the most powerful metaphors for the writer's craft ever penned, William Shakespeare offers us the story of the magician Prospero, who has the power to control natural forces—and who conjures up the title storm in *The Tempest*. Many scholars believe Shakespeare was writing of his own craft in this play—his last—and that the magician's command of nature symbolizes the writer's ability to create worlds.

The power to call up storms, raise the dead, drain oceans, set planets in orbit around newly minted suns—to create and control entire universes—is the most shamanic aspect of the writer's art. It doesn't matter that those worlds exist only on the page—to the writer and the reader, they are real enough to change lives. To become fully aware of that creative force is one of the most empowering steps a writer can take. Visualizing your creative energies as tangible entities can help you develop a full awareness of that force:

1. *See the whirlwind*. As you write, envision a whirlwind spiraling out of your hand and across a landscape. In its wake, cities rise, people

come to consciousness, lives are lived. The twister creates and destroys, alters and shapes, and you are in control of it.

2. *Absorb its power.* Picture yourself riding the whirlwind, or imagine being the whirlwind. Feel its power—which is your power—as you write. It doesn't matter whether you are writing from actual events or sheer imagination. Even if you aren't inventing the events you're writing about, you're bringing them to life.

The whirlwind is the conduit of your imagination, the funnel of your creativity. This is the force of your creative energy, your shamanic power. Pick up your pen and, as you embody the whirlwind, watch the worlds issue from your spiraling winds. Begin, "I am spinning. . . ." and keep going.

————•◦•————

Cultivating the shamanic elements in our lives can be a challenging undertaking: it asks that the writer alter his vision, his experience in the world, his way of connecting with others and the Earth. Yet when we are willing to take this path, we find it an enthralling—even life-altering—adventure. As we develop our shamanic gifts, we can often see the vision and vitality of our writing shift in marvelous, unexpected ways.

The shaman's path entails entering a different reality—whether you see that reality as an actual separate realm in which we can commune with spirits or as an altered way of viewing the world through the lens of imagination. It enables us to act as links between the mythic and the mundane, to gain knowledge and power from that other realm and bring those gifts back to the ordinary world.

But however wonderful the shamanic journey may be, we must also act as effectively as we can in the everyday world. For better or for worse, we inhabit a universe of commerce and politics, science and education, mass media and big business. We can visit the other realm, but we live in this one.

And no matter how fluent we become in the tongue of the spirits, we will fail as writers if we cannot translate it into the language of everyday life.

In the next section, we will explore a set of practical ways to face the day-to-day challenges of the writing life. The last of the writer's four sacred paths—that of the honorable warrior—offers specific ways writers can hone their skills and improve their discipline, and brings our focus to the writer as a champion of truth and a responsible citizen of the Earth.

PART IV | *The Warrior Road*

Some people find it difficult to think of warriors, with their connection to conquest and bloodshed, as a model for writers. But the warrior has been a powerful archetype throughout history. From Bushido—the way of the Japanese samurai—to the chivalric customs of the Knights of the Round Table; from the code of ancient Sparta to the Yaqui traditions Carlos Castañeda investigated, the warrior has been held up as the noblest of the human race. Today, business leaders read Wu Qi's *Art of War*, sci-fi fans emulate the "traditions" of Jedi knights, and martial arts classes are brimming with students striving to learn not just how to break bricks with their hands, but the self-control, focus, and daring of the fighter. The best aspects of the warrior—discipline, courage, and the willingness to fight for truth—are among the most admirable of virtues, and those qualities also lie at the core of the writing life.

Applying the warrior's code to writing is not a new idea. The warrior poet is an ancient notion that is still potent. In early Ireland, the *fianna*—a warrior society devoted to protecting the powerless—required that initiates be not only skilled fighters, but master poets. The legendary Odysseus was a brilliant storyteller as well as the greatest soldier of his time. Even modern-day popular culture reflects our intrigue with the warrior poet: science fiction stories and kung fu movies are heavily populated with them.

The connection between the warrior and the writer goes beyond legend and pop culture, however. Many modern writers have been both. Ernest Hemingway, Luandan novelist Artur dos Santos, and German writer Ernst Junger all wrote from their experiences in battle. The agony of war has appeared in anthologies of brilliant, edgy poems by veterans of the Vietnam and Iraq wars. The archetype also lives in writers whose battles remain on the page: Salman Rushdie and Audre Lorde have both been called warrior poets, and Maxine Hong Kingston titled her memoir *The Woman Warrior*.

One mark of a warrior is the knowledge that what she does can make a profound difference in the world. Because of that power, warriors are trained never to act recklessly or in malice. The writer, too, must live with that awareness. Like the warrior, you possess the power to alter the course of people's lives—for anything you write, no matter how trivial it seems, might change some reader's beliefs or impel her to act. That power makes you honor bound to write with the utmost integrity. If you are a writer, you are engaged in a battle for truth, justice, and peace, whether you want to be or not. This is an awesome responsibility, but learning from the warrior, studying his practices, and following his code can help us rise to the challenge.

Honor and Courage in the Writing Life

THE GREATNESS OF THE WARRIOR does not come only from her strength and daring, her skill with the sword or light saber, or her ability to vanquish her foes. It comes from the honorable way she conducts herself, from her devotion to truth and peace, from the respect she has for others, and from the courage with which she faces battle. To fulfill his greatest potential, a writer must also foster these qualities in himself. Despite the focus of writing classes, excellence in writing isn't only about voice and style. It is also about finding the truest parts of ourselves and having the moral strength never to waver from what we hold sacred. To find that strength, we can look to the warrior as a model and a guide.

Devotion to Truth

The medieval knight believed that whoever was on the side of truth would win the battle. Even if we must be more realistic today, truth is no less important now than it was a thousand years ago. But if someone asked you right now to list the basic truths you live by, could you answer? Most of us can come up with some sort of response, but it is seldom well thought out or clearly articulated. It takes some work to uncover what we truly believe in, but once we do, those truths can serve as beacons both for our daily lives and for our writing.

{ SACRED TOOL }

Finding Truth in Daily Life

We don't have to delve into dense philosophical tomes or meditate for years on the nature of reality to find truth. It is waiting for us in everyday life, in the simple experience of living as a human being. It may be easy to overlook at times—but when we allow ourselves to be present in the world, it soon emerges in sharp relief:

1. *Keep a record of your reactions.* Carry a small notebook with you for a week. Whenever you find yourself feeling annoyed or angry, write down what happened to make you feel that way. It might be when you hear a politician supporting something you virulently disagree with—or it might simply be when the guy who delivers your pizza is gruff. Just jot down a quick note and, if you have time, a word or two about how the event made you feel.

2. *Read them mindfully.* At the end of the week, sit down with your list and read it carefully several times. If you wish, write the items down

on a clean piece of paper to help you organize your thoughts. Read them with the awareness that each one of these events represents a truth for you. Even your annoyance with something as trivial as a brusque pizza delivery man may reflect your beliefs about kindness and courtesy.

3. *Identify your truths.* After studying your list carefully, identify several basic truths it reveals. Look for patterns. For example, one writer found that she'd felt upset when she saw a dog locked in a car, read an article about mistreated farm animals, and overheard someone say they had their cat euthanized because they couldn't afford to keep her. Although she'd always known that she enjoyed the presence of animals, this exercise made her realize that compassion toward our animal kin is one of the fundamental truths of her life. Sometimes you might find that a particular issue or problem appears on your list only once—but when it does, it has a particular strength or intensity. That, too, may be a sign of your truth.

Another way to clarify your truths is to write a statement about each of the events you recorded. Describe the event at the top of a sheet of paper. Below it, complete these statements:

→ "This is wrong because . . ."

→ "This can be corrected by . . ." or "The right way to do this would be to . . ."

→ "To help bring about this change, I can . . ."

Write as many completions for each statement as you wish and then go on to the next event. This can help uncover some of the beliefs and values that lie at the core of our lives.

4. *Work from positive responses.* This exercise can also be done in reverse. Instead of taking note of times when you feel angry, you can write

down experiences that made you feel especially good. Then complete these sentences:

→ "This is right because . . ."

→ "I can cultivate this type of action in my life by . . ."

However you go about this exercise, it will give you a clearer sense of what your truths are and what role you play in bringing about change in the world.

{ SACRED TOOL }

Clearing Away the Noise

We are confronted with constant information. From the minute we open the morning newspaper or turn on the traffic report to the moment we put down our mystery novel and turn out the lights at night, we are incessantly bombarded with ideas, opinions, requests, demands, and attempts to persuade us of one thing or another. Hundreds of advertisements, dozens of news reports, and scores of conversations assail us throughout the day. Amid all this racket, how can we hear the clear, quiet voice of our truth? One way is to quiet the noise—not just the noise from outside, but the internal chatter:

1. *Listen.* Sit comfortably, breathe deeply, and relax for a moment. When you feel ready, open yourself to the voices you have heard all day. Hear them: the phone calls, the meetings, the casual conversations, the news reports. Try to evoke their sounds as if they are speaking right now, all at the same time. In your mind's eye, give the voices some kind of physical form. You might imagine the faces of people whose voices you are remembering, or you can give the voices an abstract form. One writer envisioned the noise in her head as a huge swirling ball of colors. Another envisioned dozens of bubbles

floating around her head, each one babbling away. It doesn't matter if you can't make out what they are saying—there may be so many of them that they turn into one loud roar. Sit with them for a while without trying to quiet them down. Just give them time to blab.

2. *Create space.* See the voices move away from you just a little. As you do, notice the volume lowering a bit. The chatter may still be extremely noisy, but there will be a tiny space between you and the voices, and they won't be quite as loud. Again, rest with the voices and, after a time, widen that space again, see the noises moving farther away, and let the volume lower more. Continue very slowly to increase the distance between you and the noises. Keep at it until they are just a vague buzz in the distance. Stay for a while with those distant voices so that they become fixed in that far-off place. You don't necessarily have to extinguish the voices entirely. Just make them so small and far away that you can barely hear them.

3. *Wait for the quiet voice.* By now you have created a wide, open space with plenty of room for your truth to appear. Sit for a while in that space and see what comes. Don't do anything special. Don't try to beckon or even hope for something wonderful to happen—that will surely send your truth packing. Simply rest and wait patiently.

    In this spacious frame of mind, a quiet voice may appear. It may be so slight that you barely hear it at first. Don't strain to hear it. Be patient and allow it to manifest. Once it does, you will have no doubt that it is the truth you have been waiting for.

4. *Write.* Let the quiet voice inside you guide your pen and see what comes out. Don't worry about whether it is good writing—or even whether it is coherent. Just let your truth express itself. When you have finished writing, read what you have written, without placing

any expectations on yourself. Chances are that, within the jumble, there will be small gems of wisdom.

5. *Be patient.* If nothing comes to you, don't despair. It may simply not be the time for you to know your truth yet. Do the exercise again several days later. Do it as many times as you need to. Eventually, that quiet voice will speak in clear, pure tones. Listen.

These exercises can help you discover what truth means to you, but that doesn't mean that you now must set out to write political speeches or editorials about the topic. Above all, it doesn't mean that you should start infusing your stories and poems with messages. In fact, that is the poorest way to work for truth: the minute a reader spots a "moral" or "lesson" in a work of fiction or poetry, they feel cheated and talked down to. What this does mean is that, as you write the poems, stories, or essays you are called to write, you must do so with an awareness of the things you hold to be fundamentally true. Read your work with an eye to anything false or insincere, anything that makes you uncomfortable. If that discomfort comes from a violation of your basic truths, both you and your work will suffer.

COURAGE

"Fiction never exceeds the reach of the writer's courage," says *Bastard Out of Carolina* author Dorothy Allison—and the same could be said for any type of writing.[1] Courage is the first quality we think of when we envision the warrior. Surely it takes great valor to go into battle knowing that death may be waiting for you there. Writing doesn't demand that kind of immense physical bravery, but it does require great moral valor.

What is so threatening about writing? Many things are. You face the blank page knowing only you can fill it—and only if you slice into your soul. You open the deepest regions of your heart to strangers who have no reason to care. You offer the fruits of your labor, love, and struggle to agents, editors, publishers, and reviewers who will often tell you it is unworthy, feeble, pathetic. You ask those agents, editors, and publishers to risk their careers for your ideas. You face the fact that you may work for years and years without external success. You read the work of others who get published to great accolades—even when they do not write as well as you do. You have to tell everyone who asks that, no, you have not sold any of your five novels or eighteen short stories or eighty-two poems. You deal with rejection, rejection, rejection.

Writing takes another kind of courage as well. It takes courage to write the raw, unvarnished truth: to expose your most private memories, dreams, and fears; to face up to what is wrong in the world and put it on the page; and to write with utter authenticity. That is why so many of us shy away from anything ugly, sordid, or repulsive in our writing. It is also why publishers' slush piles are full of works that read false—too many of us are trying to stay on safer ground.

Fortunately, you can learn to deal with all of this fear. This is not to say that you can get rid of it entirely—or would even want to, for a certain amount of fear can be a powerful motivator—but that there are techniques for making it manageable.

———————————————{ SACRED TOOL }———————————————

Negotiating with Fear

Buddhist nun and writer Pema Chödron tells the story of a childhood friend who had a recurring nightmare about being chased by monsters. Finally, the girl dreamed that, instead of running away from the hideous creatures, she stopped and faced them. Once she looked them in the eye, the monsters began to fade away, until they disappeared completely. She never had the nightmare again.[2]

The most common reactions of writers facing fear is to hide from it or ignore it. They either avoid writing, through procrastination and blocks, or forge ahead without dealing with their feelings. In neither case are they actually confronting their fear. Imagine the fate of a warrior who slipped under a rock every time the enemy approached—or just kept marching, pretending he wasn't being shot at. The writer who just can't finish that memoir or whose writing is shallow and insincere is like that soldier. He isn't facing his worst enemy: fear.

If you think about the first step in dealing with an enemy, you will realize that it isn't attacking but negotiating. This means letting it know what you want and learning what it wants. What you want is to write your truth. What fear wants is to scare you away from that truth. Negotiating lets fear know you respect it but that it isn't going to keep you from your mission. Above all, it lets fear know that you are more powerful than it is:

1. *Stop where you are.* Writers often feel twinges of anxiety or foreboding when they write—in some cases, it gives their work an intriguing edge. But when fear starts to take over—when it is interfering with your writing instead of intensifying it, or when it is making you too uncomfortable to go on—stop right where you are. Take a deep breath and tell yourself that you are going to face your fear head-on.

2. *Address your fear directly.* Give it a formal greeting and ask it who it is. Carry on a discussion with it, either aloud or just in your head. Then listen. Don't do all the talking: give your fear time to answer you, to whimper or demand or say whatever else it wants. You can say anything you want to your fear, but the one thing you must ask is, "What do you want?" Your fear may have an answer—something you can do that will pacify it—or it may just babble nonsense. Either way, its power will weaken. Once you have stopped running, looked

it in the eye, and said its name, it will almost always shrivel up and go sniveling away.

You may be thinking, *almost* always? A surefire solution would be better. But it is important to keep in mind that not all fears are unreasonable ogres. Some are messengers from your inner self with important things to say. You might be working on something that isn't going anywhere. It may be time to start a different project. There may be an unfulfilled need in your body or soul that should be tended to—perhaps you need rest or the support of a friend. It is easy to separate these messengers from the annoying worthless fears: instead of crawling away when you face them, they will stand tall, and their words will ring true in the deepest part of you. It may take some careful observation and discernment, but you will know when to listen to your fear and when to tell it to get lost.

{ SACRED TOOL }

Diplomacy with the Demon Editor

One specific type of fear is especially difficult for writers. We can call this fear the demon editor: the voice in our head that tells us our writing is a washout, that we are just embarrassing ourselves.

This tricky entity often appears in the guise of others, especially those people we want to impress. Whether we want to admit it or not, most writers—even those of us for whom writing is a spiritual act—hope that other people will love our work, thrill to it, admire and even envy us. At the age of twenty-five—or for that matter, seventy—we are still trying to please our parents or show up the popular kids in school. And we just keep adding to the list of people we want to impress: editors who rejected our beloved poems, the two hundred agents who turned down our novel, the reviewer who called our collection of poems "mediocre." The demon editor disguises itself as these people as it belittles and derides our work.

Despite its many disguises, when you get to the core of the demon editor, you can see what it really is: you. You think you're afraid of what your father, best friend, or agent is going to think, but in large part they are just manifestations of what *you* will think. The demon editor is our own fear of inadequacy.

As with other fears, the best way of dealing with the demon editor is to confront it. But, since it is the most persistent of all fears and likely to stick around after the others have given up, we need to use a different tactic:

1. *Write a letter*. The next time you hear the unmistakable voice of the demon editor, write it a letter. Even though there's no one to actually send this letter to, put the letter down on paper to make it concrete.

2. *Unmask the demon editor*. Your letter can be as long or short as you wish and include anything you want to say, but it must do two things—unmask the demon, and tell it that you will no longer listen to it: "Stop trying to sound like my mother because you aren't her. And even if you were, I would still have to write what *I* feel is best. I will therefore not listen to anything you say about my writing from this day on."

3. *Post the letter*. Write or print the letter out and sign it. Now put it someplace handy, perhaps above your desk—because you will probably have to look at it again.

Even this tough diplomacy won't stop the demon editor once and for all, but it will quiet it down—and it gives you a resource for those times when it is growling most ferociously in your ear. When that happens, pull the letter out and read it aloud. Or simply repeat its main message: "I'm not listening to you."

Buried Treasure

Anxiety about the quality of our work is only one challenge to the writer's courage. The fear of exposure—of standing naked before the world—can be even more difficult to deal with. Writing requires us to tap our deepest secrets and to reveal the dark side of life in our communities and the world. It forces us to be painfully revealing. "A person who publishes a book willfully appears before the public with his pants down," said Edna St. Vincent Millay,[3] and anyone who has published or publicly read their work knows exactly what she was talking about.

We absolutely must not let fear of exposure keep us from writing our truth, from delving deeply into our lives and telling the stories that must be told. To deal with that fear, we must see that what we are offering the world is a treasure of immense worth. That means *all* of what we have to offer: not only the joyous and meaningful experiences but the times you lied to your best friend, cheated on an exam, or had an affair with a married man. The embarrassment, shame, eccentricities, wicked thoughts, and dishonest behavior we've engaged in may seem worthless and horrible to us, but through our writing, we make them valuable. As fiction writer Omar S. Castañeda put it, "we cloistered writers hope our wounds will be turned into pearls."[4] Visualizing those wounds and missteps as hidden treasures can help you transform the discomfort of writing about them into a liberating act:

1. *Envision your inner self as treasure.* To see your inner self—with all its neuroses, bad habits, fantasies, and dreams—as a rare gift, picture it as a treasure. Gold coins, precious gems, pearls of rare beauty, and all sorts of other wonderful bounty lie locked in a chest at the bottom of the ocean. Your mission as a warrior writer is to retrieve that cache.

2. *Remind yourself of your mission.* See the vastness of the ocean and the swell and dip of the waves. Picture the treasure lying deep below. To reach that treasure, you must have both courage and strength. You must have the vision to see it through the dark water and the confidence to know you can reach it.

3. *Set forth with courage.* You dive into the water. You feel the shock of the cold, but you do not flinch from it. You swim downward farther and farther, as deeply as you can go. You are fearful but you keep swimming. When you see the chest that contains your priceless treasure, you must unlock it. You work the lock as the water pulls you upward, your lungs still holding the air. At last, the chest falls open.

4. *Return with the treasure.* Take just a single thing—one ruby or a strand of pearls—and swim up to the surface.

5. *Write.* Keep in mind that treasure in your hand. Don't forget what you went through to claim it. Write with an awareness of its value.

Whenever you write, you hope to find the treasure within. You face the great unknown lying below the ocean surface of your self. You dive beneath the waves of everyday comings and goings into the still, dark world inside. Deep in the center, you find the wealth that is your life. Now bring it up to the surface and offer it to the world.

Going One More Step

Fantasy writer Holly Lisle has a perfect definition for courage: it is "nothing more than taking one more step than you think you can."[5] Not only does this saying capture the essence of courage, it also describes a process for finding courage in yourself:

1. *Write about whatever challenges your courage.* When you have found the topic or idea that requires courage, write about it. Whether it is something you did, a memory of something that happened to you, the fear of something that might happen, or disgust at some wrong being perpetrated on innocent beings, write about it with as much detail as possible. Give yourself plenty of time and write as quickly or slowly as feels right to you—just make sure you are not leaving anything out. Don't skip over the unpleasant facts. Don't avoid the stuff that pierces your heart.

2. *Leave your work for a time.* Put your writing down. Stick your notepad in a drawer, shut down your computer, and leave the place where you were writing. Do something pleasant that will divert your attention from the unpleasantness of the writing you just completed. Do not look at your writing for at least a full day—or longer, if you feel you need it.

3. *Read what you have written.* When the emotions that the writing has stirred in you have settled, return to it. Breathe deeply and relax. Read it all the way through on one reading. Sometimes reading aloud can make the writing come to life for you—if so, do it. When you have read your writing, ask yourself, "What is missing?" You may think that everything should already be there, since your first task was to

write with full openness and honesty, but trust me—something will be absent. If you can't find anything, read the piece again—and a third time, and a fourth. Close your eyes, breathe deeply, and meditate on what you wrote.

4. *Go one more step.* Add to what you wrote: a detail, an emotion, a nuance, anything that will bring you closer to the raw truth. Keep adding. Every time you feel yourself losing steam, say to yourself, "One more step." Continue writing.

5. *Repeat the process.* When you feel that this time you have truly written everything you can possibly say, leave your writing again. Take another day or more away from it. Then return to it. Once again, read it, asking yourself what is missing. Begin writing again, saying, "One more step. One more step."

Repeat this exercise as many times as feels right to you—but keep one thing in mind: your ego, carefully protecting itself, may try to convince you to leave the topic before it has truly been plumbed. When you sincerely feel that you have reached the core, written everything that could possibly be written and can now congratulate yourself on a job well done—that is probably when much remains to be said. Keep taking one more step.

Respecting Your Opponent

A Winnebago elder says, "We honor our veterans because by seeing death on the battlefield, they truly know the greatness of life."[6] Valuing life doesn't just mean cherishing the lives of those we love, but honoring *all* life—including our opponents'. In some warrior traditions, the victors pay homage to the valor of the foes they have defeated. To write honorably, the warrior writer must also respect his opponent.

We can accomplish this difficult shift in perspective by using our craft to help us replace blame with empathy, bravado with conviction, and aggression with connection. Several techniques can help us: writing from the viewpoint of our opponent, writing about the experiences that underlie her beliefs, and writing her life story. The use of the word *opponent* rather than *enemy* is important here. Making someone you disagree with your enemy puts her in the category of the evil, inhuman "other." It dismisses your responsibility to that person and is contrary to the idea of connection. Although there are occasionally viewpoints that we simply cannot connect with and still retain our moral compass, most of the beliefs and opinions we confront are those of sincere people who truly believe they are doing right. In most cases, it is only counterproductive to view an opponent as a demon you must crush instead of merely someone you wish to persuade or a person, group, or idea you want to challenge.

——————————————————{ SACRED TOOL }——————————————————

Writing Your Opponent's Beliefs

One of the best ways to gain respect for your opponents is to argue in favor of their beliefs, even when you deeply believe they are misguided. The point isn't to change your opinions, but to gain insight into your opponent's position and to connect with him as an honorable person who is doing what he believes best:

1. *Explore the opposing viewpoint.* Whether you have had an argument with a neighbor over whose responsibility it is to fix the sidewalk or are publicly debating nuclear proliferation, ask yourself honestly what the other side of the argument is. If your opponent is someone you know personally, you can also engage her in discussion and listen deeply to what she has to say—but if this is going to work, it

means you have to force yourself not to argue back, and that takes more self-control than most of us can muster. If you are contesting a public issue, you can find an advocacy organization for the opposing side and read their literature—many such groups can be easily found on the Internet. You can often learn about your opponents' arguments in newspaper editorials or letters to the editor.

However you go about investigating your opponents' viewpoints, try not to assess the validity of their arguments. Quiet the voice in your head that is saying, "These people are nuts! They don't even have the facts straight!" Just listen, taking in their arguments without judgment.

2. *Write for the opposing side.* When you feel you truly understand what the other side is saying, sit down and write an essay arguing for their side. Don't do this sarcastically or satirically. Write as if you honestly wanted to convince someone that your opponent is right. Use the weightiest arguments you have heard and support them with any evidence you can find. You may even discover an argument your opponent left out. Include it in your essay.

3. *Read what you have written.* When you have finished, read the essay back. As you do, try to retain an attitude of respect for the people whose viewpoints you have expressed. It is all right to believe they are wrong, but try to remember that they are people making their best efforts to understand the world and to do what is right.

Once in a great while, this exercise will sway your opinion. Other times, it will actually strengthen the beliefs you started out with. Most often, it doesn't alter your beliefs one way or the other—that isn't the point of the exercise. What it will do is help you build a healthy respect for your opponent and an ability to take their arguments as seriously as you take your own. Then you can argue your side with the valor of the warrior who respects his attackers even as he vanquishes them.

<hr/>

Writing about Your Opponent's Experiences—and Your Own

Although we like to think that our opinions are the direct result of sound reasoning, they are largely derived from the experiences we have had. If you were raised by a family of nature lovers and took many hikes when you were growing up, you're likely to be more sensitive to conservation issues than an urbanite who has never experienced the great outdoors. If you've had a loved one in prison, you will probably have different beliefs about the treatment of prisoners than if you have been the victim of a crime.

Exploring your own experiences can deepen your understanding of the source of your attitudes. Exploring the experiences that may have contributed to your opponents' point of view can help you gain empathy for those on the other side of the fence. These two things can be especially effective when done in tandem:

1. *Write your experience.* Can you think of any specific events that influenced your attitudes? Write about them in as much detail as possible. Remember that both negative and positive events can alter our perceptions—and that it sometimes only takes a single experience at a vulnerable age for us to form an opinion that will last a lifetime. For example, one writer who strongly opposed a proposal to eliminate music programs in local elementary schools recalled with great fondness his own childhood experiences with a grade school music program, which had led him to a lifelong love of music. Also keep in

mind that your experience might include the advice of a parent or someone else in authority. Dig deep and explore your history.

2. *Imagine your opponent's experience.* Now consider the person who disagrees with you. Imagine what kinds of experiences may have molded her feelings. The writer who supported the music program knew that his staunchest opponent was the mother of a learning-disabled child who needed more individual attention from his teachers and believed saving money on the music program could lead to smaller class sizes. He wrote about what it might feel like having a child who was failing at school and believing that if only the school board had enough money to hire more teachers, your child and others like him could benefit. His writing eventually became a poem about a mother's love for her child, her nagging worry, and her hopes.

3. *Create a character.* Even if you have no knowledge of your opponent's life—or if your opponent is a group of people, none of whom you know personally—you can still use your writer's imagination to envision the possible influences that formed their points of view. Create a character out of that faceless mass and give her a life with hopes and fears. One writer, embroiled in a debate about draining a wetland for development, knew her opponents only as a faceless corporation. When she first spoke of them, she used terms like "corporate greed" and "moral bankruptcy." For this exercise, she wrote a story from the point of view of a man who was still trying to prove himself to a distant father—and had always been taught that his value as a person depended on his financial success. She had no idea whether this was at the basis of her opponents' viewpoints, but the exercise at least gave a human face—and very human needs and motivations—to their actions. "I still think they're greedy bastards, and I'm going to fight them tooth and nail," she said after the exercise. "But

remembering that greed often comes out of pain made me less angry and better able to focus my energies."

Respecting Your Opponent as a Whole Human Being

One of the best ways we can come to respect our opponents is to consider them outside of the context of the issue we disagree about. When we are in a dispute with someone, we tend to see her as a stick figure. All we know about the person—or at least all we pay attention to—is the part that we disagree with. But any writer knows that all people are immensely complex and paradoxical. The obstinate coworker who is giving you a hard time for no apparent reason may also be a loving grandpa, someone who volunteers three times a week at a homeless shelter, or a veteran who fought to protect our country. The city council member who is supporting a bill you loathe may be a loving mother of three who is also caring for her aged aunt. Almost everyone has some goodness inside: even in the trial of a serial killer, defense witnesses will sometimes tell about how he helped them through difficult times. Try to see your opponent in all dimensions:

1. *Write your opponent's biography.* Write about your opponent in as much detail as you can, without referring—even a single time— to the issue that's in dispute. Do not write about the person's beliefs, write about the person: her childhood, her schooling, her family. Write about her likes and dislikes, her dreams for the future, her fears.

2. *Use your imagination.* If you don't know all this about your opponent, imagine it. Create a life for that person as you would for a character in a book. If your opponent is a group of people—a particular political

party, for example—evoke a character, give him a name (don't use "Mr. Creep E. Politician" or "Ms. Nutjob"), and write his life.

Imagine the person—real or imagined—as a whole person. Keep in mind that there are good, honest, sincere people who might see things differently from you, but who are well-meaning and caring. Describe those people kindly, with compassion, and in as much detail as you can.

These exercises force you out of the one-dimensional framework we frequently use when we disagree with someone. They are guaranteed to make you less angry and judgmental, even while your convictions remain as stalwart as ever. This work can have a powerful effect on your writing. Instead of the sweeping claims and myopic generalizations we tend to make when we see only one version of reality, we can write with greater precision and a more down-to-earth understanding. We can move from the tirade to the dialogue, from sermonizing to debate.

COMMITMENT TO PEACE

The highest tradition of the Mohawk warrior was the Great Law of Peace, a code of conduct prohibiting violence except in defensive action. One of the major treatises on Japanese ninja training exhorts the warrior to use escape rather than killing whenever he can. Martial artists of all traditions speak of the great paradox—that the ultimate goal of the honorable warrior isn't to go to war, but to protect peace. Like the warrior, the writer strives not for battle, but toward harmony, reconciliation, and peace.

One of the writer's highest goals is to express the inner workings of the human spirit in ways that evoke understanding and empathy. By making it possible for people of different regions, beliefs, and cultures to communicate, by allowing people to share each other's experiences and views of the world, the writer acts as a warrior for peace. In fact, many of the exercises already presented here aim toward greater harmony and reconciliation. Others can bring us even further toward a peaceful world.

{ SACRED TOOL }

Forging the Sword of Reconciliation

It is easy to react with knee-jerk anger when the things we believe in are challenged and what we wish for the world doesn't materialize. This does not serve us—or the things we fight for—well. Anger closes us to the possibilities for reconciliation. It prevents us from developing respect for our opponents. It creates dualistic thinking that assumes that there is only one solution to a problem. It is often neither possible nor wise to try to simply shed your anger. Instead, try transforming its white-hot energy into a useful tool.

Many writers have crafted their anger into brilliant literary works. Pat Conroy's acclaimed novel, *The Great Santini*, grew from his anger at a physically and emotionally abusive father.[7] John Grisham openly admits that he has vented his anger toward lawyers, judges, professors, and politicians in his writing, saying, "I just line 'em up and shoot 'em."[8] Sue Grafton's early mystery novels were laced with anger toward her ex-husband.[9] But to use anger as these writers have, to create rather than destroy, we need to reshape it. We need to take its intense, uncontrollable, molten metal and hammer it into a bright, sure sword. We can do this by using writing as a transformative act. This exercise is based on the premise that what you write is a manifestation of yourself, and that changing what you write can change your inner self. It can be done any time you find yourself angry about a specific issue or problem and have no constructive outlet for your anger:

1. *Prepare your molten metal and your shining sword.* For this exercise, you will need two large sheets of paper, such as the 30½ × 20½ inch

sheets available in any craft shop or art supply store. Spread them out on a large surface—the floor is fine if your desk is too small. Label one sheet "Molten Metal" and the other "Shining Sword" and draw ten fairly large circles on each sheet. Label the circles on the Molten Metal sheet with the following:

1. Aggression   6. Deadlock

2. Rage   7. Confusion

3. Victimization   8. Hostility

4. Frustration   9. Destructiveness

5. Manipulation   10. Wall Building

Now give the circles on the Shining Sword page the following labels:

1. Assertion   6. Growth

2. Energy and Passion   7. Clarity

3. Power   8. Empathy

4. Tenacity   9. Renewal

5. Authenticity   10. Creating Connection

Your Molten Metal sheet represents the state where your anger is just allowed to flow, dangerously hot and unusable. The Shining Sword sheet symbolizes the shaping of your anger into a razor-sharp weapon that can cut through destructive habits and bring clear vision and creative solutions. Note that each category on the Molten Metal sheet corresponds to a category on the Shining Sword sheet: "Aggression" to "Assertion," "Rage" to "Energy and Passion," "Victimization" to "Power," and so on.

2. *Write your feelings out.* Sit quietly and think about the issue. Let everything you feel and desire and fear come up: all the despair and rage, indignation and hope. When the emotional tension has built up, write a series of statements on a separate piece of paper expressing what you feel. (Write only on one side of the sheet—as you'll be cutting them up later.) It often works best to state the emotion you are feeling and then go into detail about what is causing you to feel that way. Here are some of the statements made by one writer, whose attempt to get an animal-protection statute passed in her city failed:

   → I feel helpless and completely humiliated. I worked for weeks on this statute—and more importantly, it would have helped animals. I can't figure out how people can be so blind.

   → I feel a horrible desire for revenge. Sometimes I imagine locking the people who voted against the statute in cages like the animals they won't help.

   → I feel very sad and discouraged. I think of suffering animals, and it breaks my heart.

   → I'm just so damned angry I could scream.

   It is important to be completely honest when you write your feelings. If you feel hatred, put it down. If you fantasize about humiliating your opponent, say it. Write for at least five minutes, letting everything out. If you run out of things to say before five minutes is up, keep your pen to the page and keep writing whatever comes up. You may discover more feelings rising to the surface if you give them time.

3. *Categorize your feelings.* When you feel you have written all you can about the issue right now, sit back, breathe, and take a moment to

regain your focus. Now read your statements—some writers find reading them out loud makes them more concrete. For each statement, decide which circle on the "Molten Metal" sheet it should go into. "I feel like I'm just going to explode" would probably go in the "Frustration" circle. "I lie in bed at night wondering what the hell to do" might fall under "Confusion." But don't get stuck on whether "I want to bash him" goes into the "Destruction" category or the "Hostility" category; just use your first thought. When you've decided where the statement belongs, cut it out and put it in the appropriate circle. Don't worry about filling all the circles—you may have many that remain empty and others that fill up with many of your statements.

Once you have placed all of your statements into the circles on the Molten Metal sheet, you have a diagram of the ways your anger is manifesting. Study it for a few minutes.

4. *Transform your feelings*. The next step is to turn all that molten metal into a shining sword by changing each expression to its positive counterpart. Work on one compartment at a time, beginning with "Aggression." Read the first sentence in the "Aggression" circle. Think of a way you could rewrite that sentence to transform it to the more controlled and constructive approach of "Assertion." Perhaps you've written, "I want to scream in this person's face that he is an idiot." That aggressive statement could be replaced with one that is more controlled and constructive, while still retaining the vitality of your original statement, such as, "I am going to write a letter telling him that I believe he is wrong, and exactly why I believe it." Rewrite your statement in its more constructive form, cut the new statement out, and put it in the "Assertion" circle on the Shining Sword sheet. Remove the original statement from the Molten Metal sheet and throw it out. Then do the next statement.

Keep going down the categories, rewriting each Molten Metal statement as a Shining Sword statement, discarding the original statement and placing the new one in the corresponding circle. In the end, all your "Aggression" statements will now be "Assertion" statements, your "Rage" statements will be "Passion and Energy" statements, your "Victimization" statements will be "Power" statements, and on through the list. Your Molten Metal sheet will be empty, and your Shining Sword sheet will be full. If you wish, paste the new statements onto the Shining Sword sheet and hang it somewhere you can see it.

This exercise can be a powerful weapon against pointless, uncontrolled anger. Once you have identified ways to transform your feelings, you can go back to the Shining Sword sheet whenever anger threatens to overtake you. Picture yourself pulling your sword out of its scabbard and holding it up. The positive energy associated with it will keep your negative anger at bay.

If you've ever written a letter to someone in an attempt to hash out something you're angry about, you know how much that anger can interfere with your writing. Most often you start off calmly expressing your feelings—and end up in a fit of rage and self-pity. That kind of rage is never useful. Rather than energizing us to write with passion, it depletes us. Instead of giving us focus, it makes us feel distracted. The goal of this exercise is not to get rid of your anger—or even to lessen it. It is to transform the uncontrollable, unwieldy form our anger often takes, to mold and focus it so that you write not as a victim, but as a warrior.

———◦———

The warrior archetype has been around for millennia, emerging and re-emerging from one era to the next in human societies around the globe. Its pervasiveness is not accidental. It stems from an intuitive awareness that to live as full human beings, we must learn the qualities of courage, honor, honesty, and dedication to peace. These qualities are beneficial for everyone. For writers, they are indispensable.

The warrior offers writers another gift: a set of techniques for honing skill and perfecting the ways we practice. In the final chapter, we will draw on the warrior archetype to enhance our focus and discipline and make our writing lives as effective as possible, giving us new avenues for developing our full potential.

{10}

Strategy and Skill for the Warrior Writer

EVERY WARRIOR KNOWS that victory depends not on mere weaponry and brute strength, but on the development of finely honed skills. For centuries, warriors of all eras and cultures have undergone years of rigorous training to develop the physical and mental prowess for success on the battlefield. The ninja of early Japan trained in no fewer than eighteen disciplines, including the use of weapons, explosives, disguise, espionage, and even geology. Medieval knights underwent fourteen years of training in warfare and chivalry, and soldiers of ancient Sparta left their families to begin formal military training at the age of seven.

Warriors train as if their lives depended on it—because they do. Writers might not literally die if they don't train well, but they *will* die artistically and spiritually. Oddly, of all artists, writers are most often the ones who overlook the value of training. Many start out with the belief that they should be at least reasonably good—if not brilliant—on their first try. No one believes she can play the piano, sing arias, or dance a lovely pas de deux without long years of preparation, but novice writers often believe that they can pen a competent first novel over the summer. Although seasoned writers know better, they seldom dedicate the kind of time and effort to training that some other artists do.

Learning to train as a warrior trains—as if your life depends on it—can be a powerful boon to the writer's work. It can expand your arsenal of skills and can help you mobilize them more readily. Perhaps more importantly, training helps you develop the warrior's two most valuable assets: solid discipline and razor-sharp focus.

Developing a Writing Strategy

On January 27, 1879, the British army confronted a contingent of Zulu warriors near Mount Isandlwana in what is now the nation of South Africa. The British, widely held to be the best-trained fighting force in the world, were armed with the most advanced technology of the time. The Zulus had spears, shields, and a few old-fashioned muskets. By the end of the day, the Zulus stood victorious and all but a handful of British troops were dead. In the century since then, dozens of theories have been proposed to explain the British defeat, but most historians agree that it was largely due to Zulu strategy.

Developing a strategic approach to writing practice means paying careful attention to what does and doesn't work, discarding techniques that weigh you down, and being constantly on the lookout for ways to improve your practice. To develop a writing strategy, you must be willing to discard old useless habits, no matter how comfortable they feel, and experiment with new techniques. You must continue to do that forever. For the writer, as for the warrior, developing a strategy is not a one-time thing, but a lifelong endeavor.

Target Practice

Imagine a soldier going into battle with only a fuzzy idea of what his objective was. He wouldn't last long. Yet writers are often unclear of what they truly want from their writing. Someone asks us why we write, and we answer with something like the worn out, "I write because I have to" or "I hope to be the best writer I can be." Both of these statements may be true, but they aren't enough. The warrior writer must know *exactly* what her goals are. Otherwise, she will have no way to plan, strategize, or focus:

1. *Brainstorm a list of your writing goals.* Don't mull and ponder—just put down as many goals as you can think of in a minute or two. Your list might include items like, "I want to learn to write dazzling prose," "I want my next novel to be a best seller," or "I want to finish the poem I'm working on right now." Sweeping and grand or restrained and humble, realistic or pie-in-the-sky—get them all down.

2. *Create a target.* On a clean sheet of paper, draw four concentric circles that look like a target, with room to write between each one. Now look at your list of goals. Focus on one of the goals and decide where it would fall among those circles. Goals that feel the most demanding *right now* should go in the center of the target. Goals that seem very remote and not very pressing should go in the outermost ring, and ones that fall between the two should be placed accordingly. For example, you may wish to establish yourself as a successful short-fiction writer, but what you are thinking about night and day is your need to revise your current story. The revision would go in the center circle and the larger goal somewhere farther from the center. When you have decided where the goal belongs, write it in the proper place and move to the next goal. Keep in mind that what goes in the center

isn't necessarily the most important goal, but the most urgent—the one you are aiming for *right now*. When you have finished, you will have a clearer understanding of what you are trying to accomplish, which tasks to work on first, and how the various goals relate to one another.

3. *Hang your target.* If you want, hang your target someplace where you can see it as a reminder of just what you are aiming for. Before you begin to write each day, look at your target. Focus on that center circle as an archer would, and remind yourself that you are aiming straight for it.

4. *Keep your target up to date.* When you accomplish a goal, reorganize your target, eliminating the one you are finished with, adding any new ones, and rearranging the target accordingly.

{ SACRED TOOL }

Your Black Belt

Before you can work on a writing strategy, you must know what successful writing is. The definition of this elusive notion will be strictly yours alone: no one else can tell you what victory means. For some, it may have to do with the number of articles they sell or the amount of money they make. Many others will base their definition on the number of pages or poems they write. Some will look to the quality, rather than quantity, of their writing. Others may evaluate success in terms of how they feel about their writing—simply feeling good about the work you have done is one form of success. You might think that because writing is your sacred path, you should have a spiritual definition of success. But what is most important is honesty. Fully acknowledging to yourself that you hope to become a highly paid magazine writer or a successful novelist—if those are what your goals are—is part of the sincerity you must have if writing is to truly be your spiritual path.

Arriving at your own definition of success is not always as clear cut as we would think it should be. Most career counselors will have you think about it logically, weighing options, and taking stock of your talents. But this often leads to what people *think* their notion of success should be—it attaches the definition to external gratification rather than to a true sense of achievement. For writers, it is often more fruitful to get at the notion of success through the deeper, more complex techniques of imagination and metaphor:

1. *Brainstorm metaphors*. Get out your writing materials and set your timer for five minutes. When you are ready, write a series of sentences beginning with, "Success is like . . ." Complete the sentence with whatever comes to mind, regardless of whether it seems to make sense. In fact, most times it won't. You might write, "Success is like the root of a redwood" or "Success is a blue balloon above a purple sky" or even, "Success is like snot." Just let the ideas flow.

   You don't have to rush through this part of the exercise, but keep going, without stopping, for the full five minutes. Above all, don't pause to think—that will just let your logical mind get in the way.

2. *Read and underline*. When the five minutes is up, take a brief breather, and then read your list. Underline a few statements that stand out as particularly meaningful to you. Again, do this without a lot of deliberation—use your first instinct.

3. *Search for patterns*. On a fresh piece of paper, write out each of the sentences you underlined. See if any patterns or consistencies appear. Patterns may emerge that you were not fully aware of. Look at the final list one writer came up with:

Success is like a beautiful bird.

Success is like the sound of a flute.

Success is like a glittering gem.

Success is like a shiny penny.

Success is like a daisy.

Now look at this writer's list:

Success is like running the marathon.

Success is like beating the train.

Success is like making it up that mountain.

Success is like putting your line in the water one more time.

As you can see, these two sets of responses are very different, and they tell us a lot about what success is for both of these writers. The interesting thing is that, before they did this exercise, both writers identified very similar goals: they both wanted to publish the short stories they were working on and, eventually, to become established fiction writers. After the exercise, their specific objectives became clearer. The first realized that he defined success in terms of small, beautiful things, such as fashioning a spell-binding scene or creating a section of sharp dialogue. The second writer's goals clearly focused more on toughness and determination. For her, success meant sticking to her plan to write for three hours a day, five days a week, and not getting derailed by rejections.

4. *Create success statements.* The final step is to turn your list into something concrete. You can do this by creating a series of statements expressing in clear-cut and specific terms what you want to accomplish, keeping in mind your metaphors for success. For example, based on this exercise, the first writer decided to reward himself whenever he finished a single, well-honed page. The second writer

saw success as completing a day's worth of writing, even when she'd just gotten a disappointing rejection or was dealing with stress in other parts of her life. Whatever you decide to make your benchmark for success, write it down in a simple affirmative sentence: "I will write ten lines of poetry every week" or "I will have a complete short story to submit to a literary journal at the end of every month" or whatever fits your definition.

5. *Put your success statements away.* Once you have written out your success statements, put them away again. Don't keep them right in front of you or you'll end up thinking more about the goals than about the writing itself. But do look at them from time to time and keep them as your own personal touchstone.

Looking for your own notion of success in this roundabout way keeps you from buying into someone else's definition or measuring your achievements against other people's. You may still wish you had many publications or lucrative book deals, but you stop lying in bed at night fretting about what your friends will think if you never publish your horror novel, and you stop thinking something must be wrong with you because you can't even sell one when Stephen King has published so many.

A second benefit of this exercise is that it prevents you from backing yourself into a corner by making your success rest on some pie-in-the-sky goal. It gets you over the novice's idea that your first novel should be a best seller, and it leads you to a real definition, something that is meaningful today. It helps keep you mindful of the fact that, just as no one tries out for his black belt in karate the first year, you must allow yourself time to practice and prepare.

Evaluating Your Process

Imagine a young man hoping to become a legendary warrior. Every morning, he rises before dawn to practice his fighting techniques. He does a variety of exercises hoping to increase his strength, stamina, and skill. He meditates and prays and even changes his diet and sleep habits. Every day, he does the same things the same way. Assuming the best method of study will simply come to him, he never stops to ask himself whether he is practicing the best way for him. He never evaluates his progress and doesn't have a clear idea of whether his method of practicing is helping or hindering him. He seldom experiments with new ways of practicing but sticks with the same techniques year after year. The young man might eventually become a warrior, but it doesn't seem very likely that he's headed for greatness.

Every writer has a process, but few ever seriously evaluate their processes. They may write early in the morning but only after having two cups of coffee, checking their email, and reading the comics. They might write late into the night or only after jogging five miles; they might always use a laptop or rely on pen and paper; they might warm up with ten minutes of freewriting or plunge right in. The writing process often becomes so ingrained that the writer doesn't know any other way to write. But, just like the young warrior-in-training in the story, writers virtually never evaluate whether they're making the best choices. They don't know whether they are doing the most effective things to help them grow and develop as writers because they've never taken stock of their processes. For the writer, as for the warrior, taking account of your process is important because it is the only way you can discover whether you're doing all you can do to develop to your full potential:

1. *Write about your writing practice.* What time of day do you write? For how long? How many breaks do you take and how long is each one?

Where do you write? What rituals do you have? What do you do when you feel stuck? What do you do when you're interrupted? Pay attention to your writing materials—perhaps you not only feel you must write on a computer, but you have to use a particular kind of mouse. Many writers have a favorite pen or type of paper. If you are one of the rare writers who writes differently every day, write about that—even having a very free, open approach is a kind of process. Be thorough, specific, and detailed.

2. *Test your process step by step.* Once you have gotten your process out in the open, you can begin working with it. Try altering one aspect, keeping everything else the same. If you usually write only in your office with the door shut, try going to a café or a park. If you always write for two hours in the morning, try writing in the afternoon or evening. Even if it feels annoying and unnatural—and it probably will—give it a try and make yourself stay at it at least for a day or so. The point is to experiment with your writing practice in a structured way, and to test out whether your writing habits are actually aiding or hindering you.

3. *Evaluate.* At the end of the day, write briefly about how the change affected your writing. Did you write more or less than usual? Did you find the words coming more easily or did they seem stuck? Did you feel better after you wrote than you usually do, or did you feel worse? Did you move toward achieving the goal you set in your success statement?

4. *Continue experimenting.* Next, change a different aspect: this time, perhaps you'll try a pad and pen instead of your trusty computer, or maybe you'll do yoga after you write instead of before. As before, stick to the change for at least a day and evaluate it afterward through freewriting. Repeat this process, altering one thing at a time.

5. *Conclude with an overall evaluation of your process.* At the end of this experiment, bring out each of the end-of-day descriptions that you wrote. Read them carefully to get an overall understanding of whether any of the changes in your process sparked a change in your writing. You may find that your old process was definitely the best one and go back to it with renewed awareness. Or you may be surprised to find that some of the changes you've made stimulated your writing in ways you didn't expect. Some writers discover that they want to switch back and forth, for example, by writing at home some days and at the park the next.

This exercise makes you conscious of your process as a set of choices rather than an imperative you must follow. It jars you out of your writing complacency and challenges you to try something new. Even if you find your old system works the best, you will go back to it with greater insight into what does and does not benefit your writing.

{ SACRED TOOL }

Continuing to Build Successful Strategies

No warrior learns a single strategy and then refuses to learn anything else. An expert fighter continually experiments, perfecting established strategies, discarding old ones when they've found something better, and trying out things just to see if they'll work. A warrior who used the same unsuccessful strategy over and over wouldn't last long on the battlefield—and the writer who does the same might undermine her writing for years.

When you have clearly determined what success means to you and what your best process is, evaluate your strategies on a regular basis. Once a month works best:

1. *Do a monthly review.* At the end of each month, take stock by writing a review of your accomplishments for the previous four weeks. Your review can be free-flowing and meandering or carefully structured, but it should answer a number of questions:

    ➻ Did you meet the goal articulated in your success statement? If not, how close did you come? If you exceeded your goal, how far beyond it did you go?

    ➻ Did you stick with your process? If not, what did you change?

    ➻ How do you feel about the writing you did this month? What emotions come up around your work?

2. *Allow your goals to change.* It is not uncommon for writers to discover that their goals have changed in the process of writing over the previous month. Perhaps you started out with the goal of writing five poems. Instead, you wrote only one—but that one is a dazzling gem, your best work ever. It would be ridiculous for you to decide you'd failed because the goal you set up four weeks ago was never met. Be flexible and give yourself credit.

3. *Study your failures.* Perhaps you definitely feel that you didn't accomplish what you should have this month. Don't be discouraged—remember that a martial artist might try out for a belt many times before succeeding. The important thing is to determine *why* you didn't meet your goal. Ask yourself these questions:

    ➻ Was the goal unrealistic?

    ➻ Did your commitment to your process flag at any point? Did you skimp on your writing time or neglect some aspect of your usual writing practice? Did you take days off because you just didn't feel like writing or distract yourself by checking your email every ten minutes?

➤ Did something happen—a problem at home or at work, for example—that interfered with your focus?

4. *Consider possible modifications.* If you answer no to these questions, it is likely that you aren't using the best strategy. Think about ways you could change it. If you aren't sure what would work better (and we often don't know until we try), go back to the "Evaluating Your Process" exercise to come up with a new process. Then set a new goal, try your new process out for a week or longer, and see what happens.

If you did achieve your goal for the month, recommit to your process. If you have found that writing for two hours in the afternoon, four times a week has worked for you, remind yourself that this is your process and affirm that you are going to stick with it.

No-Mind

When Daniel Kohn—a rabbi with a black belt in aikido—found himself facing several opponents coming at him from all directions, he had no time to think. He describes experiencing a state of "complete emptiness" in which he responded not rationally, but with sudden intuitive insight.[1] This spontaneous awareness is what renowned Tibetan Buddhist teacher Chögyam Trungpa was referring to when he taught his student, Allen Ginsberg, the phrase "first thought, best thought" as a key to writing practice.[2] This is the state of *no-mind*: the spontaneous clarity of the warrior in battle—or the swift, perfect action of an ordinary person reacting heroically to an emergency.

The most essential quality of the state of no-mind is that it does not involve planning, reasoning, or thinking things through. To engage it, we have to get past the part of ourselves that wants to interpret and analyze. This elusive state of mind isn't easy to achieve, but some unusual practices can help get you there.

Multitasking

One way to get past the rational mind as we write is to keep it busy. As counterintuitive as this seems, writing while we simultaneously focus on something else can help us bypass our analytical side. This exercise can also be a bit crazy making, but accepting the challenge with a sense of humor is an interesting way to work toward the no-mind state:

1. *Doing two things at once.* Practice writing as you are engaged in some task that requires you to think—a little:

   → Singing a song

   → Counting

   → Reciting the alphabet

   → Spelling words out loud

2. *Set the right level of challenge.* There are many other possibilities, but remember that the task must require the right amount of mental work. Something too difficult, such as doing arithmetic problems, will stop most writers in their tracks, while something too easy, like counting from one to five, might not pose enough of a challenge.

This exercise is hardly the best way to do detailed revision—but it is an excellent way to short-circuit the analytic part of your brain and get to the spontaneity and creativity of no-mind.

Writing with Zen Koans

Most of us have heard of koans, those quirky, nonsensical sayings, like "the sound of one hand clapping," that practitioners of Zen use to break through the rational mind. People in the West tend to dismiss them or take the attitude that if they only think hard enough, they will come up with an explanation. Neither is the right approach. Koans are meant to channel energy away from the rational part of our minds, to force us to consider something that *can't* be analyzed. We can use koans to help us break through to the no-mind state in our writing.

1. *Pick a koan to work with.* A few are listed below, and many more can be found in books on Zen, or online. Pick one, read it once, and start writing:

    → When you meet a woman on the way, greet her without words, greet her without silence. How will you greet her?

    → The Zen sage Shuzan held out his short staff and said, "If you call this a short staff, you oppose its reality. If you do not call it a short staff, you ignore the fact. Now what do you wish to call this?"

    → The world is vast and wide. Why do you put on your robes at the sound of a bell?

    → The flag doesn't move; only your mind moves.

2. *Work from your first thought.* Remember Chogyam Trungpa's words to Allen Ginsberg—"first thought, best thought." Let your first thought take you where it will. Don't think or analyze.

3. *Keep returning to the koan.* You will find that you start your rational thinking processes by the time you've written a few words. To prevent them from taking over, go back to the koan at a specific interval—every first, second, or third line works well for most writers. When you return to the koan, drop what you are writing immediately and start the next line with the same koan.

Here is an example of writing from a koan. In this case, the writer started the koan—"The flag doesn't move, only your mind moves," repeating it with every new line:

> *The flag doesn't move only your mind moves swiftly running carrying over*
>
> *The flag doesn't move only your mind moves where is it will it go far where*
>
> *The flag doesn't move only your mind moves how how how how and why*
>
> *The flag doesn't move only your mind moves your mind moves over the rocks*
>
> *The flag doesn't move only your mind moves your mind like a bird*
>
> *The flag doesn't move only your mind moves the bird like a white cloud*
>
> *The flag doesn't move only your mind moves the bird like a white flag*
>
> *The flag doesn't move, only your mind moves, your mind like a white bird like a white flag.*

These lines—which could be the first draft of a poem—were written in less than a minute. Reading them back, you can almost follow the writer's rational mind trying to take over, and see the return to nonrational thinking with each new repetition of the koan.

MASTERY THROUGH DISCIPLINE

The highest goal of warrior training is mastery. This ultimate objective is not mere knowledge or skill, but an understanding that comes only from getting to the very core of an activity. According to Taoist philosopher Zhuangzi, mastery occurs only when an activity becomes part of your very self. Of course with writing, as with the skills of the warrior, you could spend many lifetimes going deeper and deeper into the heart of the endeavor, so mastery is always an ongoing process. But the awareness that you are on the way to that ultimate goal—that you have gone beyond mere skill into the deeper aspects of your art—provide a deep sense of assurance and confidence.

There is only one route to mastery: discipline. Anyone who has seriously taken up writing knows the value of this essential quality. Yet writers often overlook some important forms of discipline. They consider it enough to write every day, avoid procrastination, and complete projects rather than letting them dangle. Of course, those forms of discipline are important, and if you haven't yet developed them, you should. But there are other forms of writing discipline that can help you move toward mastery.

Mastering Form

When martial artists train, they don't just learn to blindly attack. They study specific movements, postures, and stances, which they practice many thousands of times until they are second nature. The *kata* of karate, the *hyung* of tae kwon do, and the *quyen* of Vietnamese martial arts are all based on the same principle: training the body to perform precise, controlled forms through years of repetition.

Many artists—dancers, musicians, painters, and actors—also study their own sort of *kata*: techniques that serve as the foundation of their craft. They work under masters and practice assiduously for many years to perfect these building blocks. It is impossible to imagine a great pianist who never worked on scales, or a ballet dancer who hadn't learned the five basic ballet positions. Artists eventually go far beyond the techniques they have learned, but only after they have complete control of them.

In contrast, some writers pay little attention to technique. They believe they can beautifully write without ever learning form and structure. The dexterous use of words, a command of metaphor and tropes, and skill at manipulating sentence melody all form the foundations of writing. Practicing these techniques the way a warrior practices form—not just a few times, but over and over until they are so natural that they come without thought—is basic to developing mastery:

1. *Pick a specific technique to use as kata practice.* There are many possibilities to choose from:

    → The basic forms of poetry. Get a good book on poetry or look up the forms online. You will find many: haiku and odes, pantoums and villanelles, sonnets and sestinas, and dozens more.

→ Poetic devices, such as alliteration, assonance, metaphor, and metonymy.

→ Segments of dialogue.

→ Paragraphs, short scenes, or very short stories (under one hundred words).

2. *Develop skill through repetition.* Whatever you pick, practice it as a martial artist practices *kata.* Say you have decided to practice haiku—a good way to develop skill at precise, succinct language. Don't just write two or three haiku and move on to something else. Remember the martial artist repeating the same movement again and again, and follow her example. Write several haiku every day for weeks as part of your writing practice. You might do it as a daily warm-up, as a cool-down at the end of your writing practice, or as a breather when you need a break from your other writing work—but do it over and over until it seems ridiculous to keep working on it, then work on it some more. Think of yourself as working toward your black belt in writing—the only way to get there is to have the discipline to keep at the hard work. Get to the point where that terse, clean language seems like a part of you. Then move on to another form and do the same.

This kind of discipline forces you to concentrate on the rhythm and resonance of words. It teaches precision. It makes you focus. And it can serve as the basis for writing discipline throughout your life. Just as karate masters continue to practice *kata,* the writer's work on form should continue as long as he is writing.

Learning from Masters

A martial artist may study with a teacher throughout her life. Similarly, writers can and should learn from master writers. Most writers read the works of authors they want to emulate, and many borrow from them. But few writers seriously study the work of an expert writer or attempt to incorporate his techniques in their own writing. Rather than simply reading and admiring excellent work, use this structured plan for learning from masters:

1. *Study the work of a master.* Pick a writer whom you especially admire. From the writer's works, select a passage—a substantial paragraph or scene—and read it carefully, not once, but over and over. You might incorporate into your practice the reading of this single passage every morning. Read it aloud and read it silently. If you want, record your voice reading it and listen to it. Type or write the passage out over and over. You can even memorize the passage, if you wish.

2. *Let the passage resonate.* When you know the passage so well you can feel it in your bones, let it ring inside you. Don't try to analyze it or figure out why it works, just let its effect flow through you and establish itself inside of you. Do this for several days.

3. *Do a writing meditation on the passage.* As in all meditative writing, let your thoughts go where they may. You might write about how you feel when you read the passage, particular things about it that resonate with you, or things you want to learn from it. See what comes up.

This exercise leads to subtle but real shifts in the quality of your writing. It allows an intuitive understanding of what makes for good writing to sink in, to get into your bones. Often, you will find the strengths you admired emerging in your own writing—sometimes when you least expect it.

Mastering Focus

In the "Evaluating Your Process" and "Continuing to Build Successful Strategies" exercises, we talked about finding writing practices that work for you by evaluating your process and altering it when necessary. The idea was to do away with strategies that don't work and find ones that do. But you can also use strategies that *don't* work for you as a way of challenging and improving your focus:

1. *Pick a strategy that doesn't work well.* Perhaps you have tried writing in a crowded café and know that you just don't do as well there as in your solitary office. Or maybe you've found that you're much less productive in the afternoon than at your usual writing time at 6:00 A.M. Pick one strategy that doesn't feel natural or right for you.

2. *Force yourself to write using that strategy.* Try staying at that café or keeping to your later schedule. Face the challenges that those shifts in your practice confront you with. Is there too much noise? Try working through it. Do you feel sleepy in the afternoon? Try writing then anyway. Do you find writing with a pen too slow now that you're used to a keyboard? Work against that feeling—not by trying to match the speed of your keyboard, but by dealing with the slowness. Accept that you are writing with a pen and that it annoys and frustrates you, but do it anyway.

The point of this exercise is to increase your ability to focus on your writing. When we are developing physical strength, we don't go with the one thing that works easily—we challenge ourselves. We add extra weight to our dumbbells, more incline to our walk, more repetitions of an exercise. If we find that we're particularly weak in an area, we work on it specifically. This exercise operates the same way. It strengthens our focus—and our resolve—by putting extra weight or tension on it. When we go back to the strategies that we find most comfortable, we bring that fortified focus with us.

—————◆•◆•◆—————

Throughout these exercises, it is helpful to remember that discipline isn't simply a matter of forcing ourselves to do something or trying hard to achieve goals. True discipline doesn't come from our attempts to get a novel published or make more money. It comes from the conviction that we want to live our lives as writers. According to martial arts expert F. J. Chu, the warrior "transforms everything he does into an act of training."[3] This is another way writers are like warriors. Not only can we work on specific training techniques like those presented in this chapter, but we find training opportunities in everything that happens. We turn every action we take, every thought we think, every moment we live, into an education in writing.

Walking the Sacred Path

IN 1971, I SPENT THE NIGHT at a Shinto shrine in southern Japan. I was backpacking through the country and had stumbled across this small holy place dedicated to the *kami*—the spirit or soul—of the bay upon which it sat. It was a lovely spot, set in a misty grove of cypresses.

At sunset, the priest of the shrine appeared and began to perform one of his evening rituals, and we struck up a conversation. He suggested that rather than going back into town to look for a hotel, I throw my sleeping bag on the floor of the shrine. The weather was mild and, he assured me, the *kami* wouldn't mind. The next morning, the young priest served me breakfast and talked about his faith.

Everything, he said, possesses *kami*: rocks, trees, birds, the stars, the wind. As a priest, his duty was to act as an emissary for them, especially for that of the bay. He communicated to her and passed her messages along to whomever needed them. If he listened carefully, he would know what she wanted to say. His job was hard, he told me. He had to perform daily rituals and keep the shrine spotless, all the while making sure he knew what the *kami* wanted. But he had been entrusted with a holy task and would never think of doing anything else.

I have thought of that priest many times through my writing life. I have often imagined myself—and all writers—to be like him. We have been given the task of serving the living and nonliving world around us, to act as representatives of the Earth and all its inhabitants, to give them voice. We are the story catchers. Like the Shinto priest, we are heirs to a tradition stretching far back into the past, the descendants of the first storytellers and of all the writers who came before us. We must diligently tend our shrines. We, too, have been entrusted with sacred work.

The four paths explored in this book are gateways to doing that work mindfully and with an open heart. From the mystic, we can learn to write with the spontaneous creativity of flow and to set aside conventional thinking to develop our own unique perspectives. The monk can teach us to grow our writing both by fostering silence in our lives and by deepening our relationships with others. From the shaman, we can learn how to journey in the realm of memory, imagination, myth, and dream, and how to draw energy from our relationship with the natural world. The warrior can show us how to be brave and honorable, focused and disciplined.

These four gateways are just a beginning. As you continue to walk the writer's path, following whatever fork in the road calls to you, remember always that the opportunity to write is a gift that comes with great responsibility. It is not ours to keep—we will eventually pass it on to others—but while we are on Earth, it is in our hands and we must care for it. That realization will keep you writing no matter what storms blow through your life and will make your writing authentic, courageous, and rooted in truth.

ENDNOTES

Chapter 1: The Call

1. John F. Baker, "Starling Lawrence: Editor to Spare-Time Novelist," *Publisher's Weekly* 244, no. 32 (1994): 51.

2. Pierre Nordon, *Conan Doyle*, trans. Frances Partridge (London: John Murray, 1966), 172.

3. "Questions Students Often Ask Elaine Marie Alphin," http://members .aol.com/elainemalphin/Alphin_FAQ.html.

4. PBS Online, "The Martyrdom of Saints Perpetua and Felicitas," *Frontline: From Jesus to Christ*, www.pbs.org/wghb/pages/frontline/ shows/religion/ maps/primary/perpetua.html.

5. George Plimpton, *The Writer's Chapbook: A Compendium of Fact, Opinion, Wit, and Advice from the Twentieth Century's Preeminent Writers* (New York: Viking, 1989), 34.

6. Matthew the Poor, *Orthodox Prayer Life: The Interior Way* (Yonkers, NY: St. Vladimir's Seminary Press, 2003), 25.

7. Patrice Vecchione, *Writing and the Spiritual Life: Finding Your Voice by Looking Within* (Chicago: Contemporary Books, 2001), 138.

8. Thomas Merton, *Blaze of Recognition*, ed. Thomas P. McDonnell (Garden City, NY: Doubleday, 1983), 124.

9. Helen V. Zahara, "The Placid Lake of the Mind," in *Approaches to Meditation*, ed. Virginia Hanson (Wheaton, IL: The Theosophical Publishing House, 1976), 68.

10. Vecchione, *Writing*, 138.

Chapter 2: The Sacred Gift

1. Andrew Turnbull, *Scott Fitzgerald* (New York: Scribner's, 1962), 259.

2. E. B. White, "The Ring of Time," in *Modern American Prose*, eds. John Clifford and Robert DiYanni (New York: McGraw Hill, 1993), 487.

3. Anaïs Nin. *The Diaries of Anaïs Nin*, vol. 5., (1947–1955) (Orlando, FL: Harvest/HBJ Books, 1975), 171.

4. R. L. LaFevers, "The Creative Process," www.rllafevers.com/for_writers .html (accessed January 17, 2008).

5. Barry Lopez, *Crow and Weasel* (New York: Farrar, Straus and Giroux, 1998), 48.

6. Omar S. Castañeda, personal communication to the author, 1988.

Part I: The Mystic Journey

1. Kena Upanishad 1:3–4.

2. Percy Bysshe Shelley, "Defense of Poetry," *Modern History Sourcebook*, www.fordham.edu/halsall/mod/shelley-poetry.html (accessed December 19, 2007).

3. Constantine Fitzgibbon, *The Life of Dylan Thomas* (London: J. M. Dent & Sons, 1966), 87.

Chapter 3: Transcendent Awareness

1. Susan K. Perry, *Writing in Flow: Keys to Enhanced Creativity* (Cincinnati, Writer's Digest Books, 2001), 1.

2. Anne Lamott, *Bird by Bird: Some Instructions on Writing and Life* (New York: Anchor, 1995), 17.

3. St. Teresa of Avila, *Interior Castle, or The Mansions,* ed. F. Benedict Zimmerman (Whitefish, MT: Kessenger Publishing, 2003), 244.

4. AtlanticMonthly.com, "A Conversation with Tess Gallagher," *The Atlantic Unbound*, July 1997, www.theatlantic.com/unbound/interviews/ interviews.htm.

5. AtlanticMonthly.com, "A Conversation with Christina Adam," *The Atlantic Unbound*, November 1996, www.theatlantic.com/unbound/interviews/interviews.htm.

Chapter 4: Crazy Wisdom

1. Demetri Dimas Efthyvoulos, "Reflections of Rainforest Spirits," *Shaman's Drum* 72 (2006): 32–37.

2. Wes Nisker, *The Essential Crazy Wisdom* (Berkeley, CA: Ten Speed Press, 2001), 10.

3. Emily Dickinson, *The Complete Poems of Emily Dickinson*, ed. Thomas H. Johnson (Boston: Back Bay Books, 1976), 506.

4. Edward de Bono, *Lateral Thinking: Creativity Step by Step* (New York: Harper, 1973).

5. Joseph Goldstein, *One Dharma: The Emerging Western Buddhism* (New York: HarperCollins, 2003), 99–100.

Part II: The Monastic Path

1. Thomas Merton, *The Monastic Journey*, ed. Brother Patrick Hart (Kansas City: Sheed Andrews and McMeel, Inc., 1977), 5.

Chapter 5: The Writer in Silence and Solitude

1. Michael Ventura, "The Talent of the Room," *LA Weekly* (May 1993): 22, www.laweekly.com.

2. Virginia Woolf, *A Room of One's Own* (Orlando, FL: Harcourt, 1991), 2.

3. Marguerite Duras, *Writing*, trans. Mark Polizzotti (Cambridge, MA: Lumen Editions, 1998), 2.

4. Wayne E. Oates, *Nurturing Silence in a Noisy Heart* (Minneapolis, MN: Augsburg Fortress Publishers, 1996), 37.

5. Michael Stocker, "Sound and the Subconscious," *Hear Where We Are*, Michael Stocker Associates, www.msa-design.com (accessed July 2, 2006).

6. Oates, *Nurturing Silence*, 61.

7. Jacques Castermane, "An Inner Experience," *UNESO Courier* (1996): 32.

8. William Penn House, www.williampennhouse.org (accessed December 12, 2008).

9. Donald M. Murray, "One Writer's Curriculum," *The English Journal* 80, no. 4 (1991): 17.

10. Murray, "Curriculum," 17.

Chapter 6: The Writer in Community

1. Fitzgibbon, *Dylan Thomas*, 10.

2. Worth Abbey, "Monasticism Today," www.worth.org.uk/guides/m8.

3. Buddhist monk at Eiheiji Monastery, personal communication to the author, 1971.

4. Ralph Keyes, *The Courage to Write: How Writers Transcend Fear* (New York: Henry Holt, 1995), 83.

5. Adi Granth, Ramkali-ki-Var, M.1, (Amritsar, India: Shiromani Gurdwara Parbandhak Committee, 1983).

6. James 1:22 (New American Standard).

7. Kahlil Gibran, *The Prophet* (New York, Knopf, 1922), 6.

Part III: The Way of the Shaman

1. Mircea Eliade, *Shamanism: Archaic Techniques of Ecstasy*, trans. Willard R. Trask (Princeton, NJ: Princeton University Press, 1964), 148, 330, 337.

2. Joan Halifax, *Shamanic Voices: A Survey of Visionary Narratives* (New York: Penguin, 1979), 3.

3. AtlanticMonthly.com, "A Conversation with Sheila Gordon," *The Atlantic Unbound*, December 1996, www.theatlantic.com/unbound/factfict/sgordon.htm.

4. Tim O'Brien, "The Magic Show," in *Writers on Writing*, eds. Robert Pack and Jay Parini (Hanover, VT: Middlebury College Press, 1991), 175.

Chapter 7: Darkness and Healing on the Writer's Path

1. Laurie Robertson-Lorant, *Melville: A Biography* (New York: Clarkson-Potter, 1996), 171.

2. Linda Richards, "Clive Barker Comes Out: An Intimate Visit with One of the Masters of Scary Stuff," *January Magazine*, www.januarymagazine.com/barker.html (accessed June 5, 2008).

3. PBS Online, *NOW*, "Transcript: Bill Moyers Interviews Isabel Allende," www.pbs.org/now/transcript/transcript_allende.html (accessed June 13, 2003).

4. Naomi Epel, *Writers Dreaming* (New York: Vintage, 1994), 212.

5. Bill Moyers, introduction to *The Power of Myth*, by Joseph Campbell (New York: Anchor, 1991), xii.

6. Matt Haig, "Why Writers Are Miserable," *Penguin [Blog] U.S.A.* (February 4, 2008), www.us.penguingroup.com/static/html/blogs/why-writers-are-miserable-matt-haig.

7. Julie Baumgold, "Fellow Traveler: Blending Fact and Fiction with Paul Theroux," *Esquire*, September 1,1996, www.encyclopedia.com/doc/1G1-18656274.html.

8. Robertson-Lorant, *Melville*, 172–173.

9. Cynthia Leitich Smith, "Rituals," *Cynsations* (July 14, 2004), www.cynthialeitichsmith.blogspot.com/2004/07/rituals.html.

10. George Plimpton, *The Writer's Chapbook: A Compendium of Fact, Opinion, Wit, and Advice from the Twentieth Century's Preeminent Writers* (New York: Viking, 1989), 54.

11. Adán Griego, "The Wandering Spirits of Isabel Allende," www.isabelallende.com/interviews_articles.htm (accessed November 10, 2007).

12. Emily Brontë, "The Old Stoic," *Poets Corner*, www.theotherpages.org/poems/bronte01.html (accessed January 4, 2008).

13. Epel, *Writers*, 92.

14. Maisah Robinson, "Gwendolyn Brooks: First African American to Receive Pulitzer Prize," *Suite 101*, February 11, 2001, www.suite101.com/article.cfm/african_american_history/60161.

Chapter 8: Sacred Ground

1. Maxine Hong Kingston, personal communication to the author, 1986.

2. Juliet Harding, "Online Interviews with Gary Snyder," *Modern American Poetry* (n.d.), www.english.uiuc.edu/maps/poets/s_z/snyder/interviews.htm.

3. Cheryl Lander, "EarthSaint: Annie Dillard," *EarthLight Magazine* 24 (Winter 1997), www.earthlight.org/earthsaint24.html.

4. Susan Salter Reynolds, " 'Our World' by Mary Oliver," *Los Angeles Times*, January 6, 2008, www.latimes.com/features/books/la-bk-reynolds6jan06,0,5486849.story.

5. Alden Mudge, "Guterson Offers a Moving Story of One Man's Final Pilgrimage," *First Person Book Page*, www.bookpage.com/9904bp/david_guterson.html (accessed January 9, 2008).

6. William Wordsworth, "The Table Turned," www.poetryfoundation.org (accessed May 8, 2008).

7. Ann Wendland, "The Next Thoreau: Place-Based Essays with the Power to Change Us," *The Exchange* (Winter 2004): 6.

8. Barry Lopez, *Crossing Open Ground* (New York: Vintage Press, 1989), 65.

9. Andrew Goatley, "The Representation of Nature on BBC World Service," *Text* 22, no.1 (2002): 1–27.

Part IV: The Warrior Road

Chapter 9: Honor and Courage in the Writing Life

1. Dorothy Allison, *Skin: Talking about Sex, Class, and Literature* (Ann Arbor, MI: Firebrand Books, 2005), 217.

2. Pema Chödron, *When Things Fall Apart: Heart Advice for Difficult Times* (Boston: Shambhala, 2000), 28–29.

3. "Edna St. Vincent Millay," *Famous Poets and Poems*,
   www.famouspoetsandpoems.com/poets/edna_st__vincent_millay
   (accessed May 8, 2008).

4. Omar S. Castañeda, *Naranjo the Muse* (Houston, TX: Arte Publico,
   1997), iv.

5. Holly Lisle, "Everyday Courage and the Writer," *HollyLisle.com*,
   www.hollylisle.com/fm/articles (accessed October 10, 2007).

6. Tom Holm, "PTSD in Native American Vietnam Veterans: A
   Reassessment," *Wicazo Sa Review* 11, no. 2 (1995): 85.

7. Keyes, *Courage*, 70.

8. Keyes, *Courage*, 83.

9. Linda Richards, "'G' Is for Grafton: Sue Grafton's Murderous Moments,"
   January Magazine, www.januarymagazine.com/grafton.html (accessed
   May 8, 2008).

Chapter 10: Strategy and Skill for the Warrior Writer

1. Daniel Kohn, *Kinesthetic Kabbalah: Spiritual Practices from Martial Arts
   and Jewish Mysticism* (Charleston, SC: BookSurge Publishing, 2004)
   9–10.

2. Allen Ginsberg, *Spontaneous Mind: Selected Interviews, 1958–1996*, ed.
   David Carter (New York: Harper, 2002), 406; Richard Modiano, "First
   Thought-Best Thought," *Poetix*, www.poetix.net (accessed June 5,
   2008).

3. F. J. Chu, *The Martial Way and Its Virtues: The Tao De Gung* (Wolfeboro,
   NH: YMMA Publication Center, 2003), 12.

Bibliography

Allison, Dorothy. *Skin: Talking about Sex, Class, and Literature*. Ann Arbor, MI: Firebrand Books, 2005.

AtlanticMonthly.com. "A Conversation with Tess Gallagher." *The Atlantic Unbound*. www.theatlantic.com/unbound/interviews/interviews.htm, July 1997.

———. "A Conversation with Christina Adam." *The Atlantic Unbound*. www.theatlantic.com/unbound/interviews/interviews.htm, November 1996.

———. "A Conversation with Sheila Gordon." *Atlantic Unbound Interviews*. www.theatlantic.com/unbound/factfict/sgordon.htm, December 1996.

Baker, John F. "Starling Lawrence: Editor to Spare-Time Novelist." *Publisher's Weekly* 244, no. 32 (1994): 51–52.

Baumgold, Julie. "Fellow Traveler: Blending Fact and Fiction with Paul Theroux." *Esquire* (Sep. 1, 1996). www.encyclopedia.com/doc/1G1-18656274.html.

Castañeda, Omar S. *Naranjo the Muse*. Houston, TX: Arte Publico, 1997.

Castermane, Jacques. "An Inner Experience." *UNESCO Courier* (May 1996): 32.

Chödron, Pema. *When Things Fall Apart: Heart Advice for Difficult Times*. Boston: Shambhala, 2000.

Chu, F. J. *The Martial Way and Its Virtues: The Tao De Gung*. Wolfeboro, NH: YMMA Publication Center, 2003.

de Bono, Edward. *Lateral Thinking: Creativity Step by Step*. New York: Harper, 1973.

Duras, Marguerite. *Writing*. Translated by Mark Polizzotti. Cambridge, MA: Lumen Editions, 1998.

"Edna St. Vincent Millay." *Famous Poets and Poems*. www.famouspoetsandpoems.com/poets/edna_st_vincent_millay.

Efthyvoulos, Demetri Dimas. "Reflections of Rainforest Spirits." *Shaman's Drum* 72 (Winter 2006): 32–37.

Eliade, Mircea. *Shamanism: Archaic Techniques of Ecstasy*. Translated by Willard R. Trask. Princeton, NJ: Princeton University Press, 1964.

Epel, Naomi. *Writers Dreaming*. New York: Vintage, 1994.

Fitzgibbon, Constantine. *The Life of Dylan Thomas*. London: J. M. Dent & Sons, 1966, 87.

Gibran, Kahlil. *The Prophet*. New York: Knopf, 1922.

Ginsberg, Allen. *Spontaneous Mind: Selected Interviews, 1958–1996*. Edited by David Carter. New York: Harper, 2002.

Goatley, Andrew. "The Representation of Nature on BBC World Service." *Text* 22, no.1 (2002): 1–27.

Haig, Matt. "Why Writers Are Miserable." *Penguin* [Blog]. www.us.penguingroup.com/statis/html/blogs/why-writers-are-miserable-matt-haig.

Halifax, Joan. *Shamanic Voices: A Survey of Visionary Narratives*. New York: Penguin, 1979.

Harding, Juliet. "Online Interviews with Gary Snyder." *Modern American Poetry*. www.english.uiuc.edu/maps/poets/s_z/snyder/interviews.htm.

Holm, Tom. "PTSD in Native American Vietnam Veterans: A Reassessment." *Wicazo Sa Review* 11, no. 2 (1995): 83–86.

Keyes, Ralph. *The Courage to Write: How Writers Transcend Fear*. New York: Henry Holt, 1995.

Kohn, Daniel. *Kinesthetic Kabbalah: Spiritual Practices from Martial Arts and Jewish Mysticism*. Charleston, SC: BookSurge Publishing, 2004.

LaFevers, R. L. "The Creative Process." www.rllafevers.com/for_writers.html.

Lamott, Anne. *Bird by Bird: Some Instructions on Writing and Life*. New York: Anchor, 1995.

Lander, Cheryl. "EarthSaint: Annie Dillard." *Earthlight Magazine* 24 (Winter 1997). www.earthlight.org/earthsaint24.html.

Lisle, Holly. "Everyday Courage and the Writer." *HollyLisle.com*. www.hollylisle.com/fm/articles.

Lopez, Barry. *Crow and Weasel*. New York: Farrar, Straus and Giroux, 1998.

———. *Crossing Open Ground*. New York: Vintage Press, 1989.

Matthew the Poor. *Orthodox Prayer Life: The Interior Way*. Yonkers, NY: St. Vladimir's Seminary Press, 2003, 25.

Merton, Thomas. *The Monastic Journey*. Edited by Brother Patrick Hart. Kansas City: Sheed Andrews and McMeel, Inc., 1977.

———. *Blaze of Recognition*. Edited by Thomas P. McDonnell. Garden City, NY: Doubleday, 1983.

Moyers, Bill. Introduction to *The Power of Myth*, by Joseph Campbell. New York: Anchor, 1991.

Mudge, Alden. "Guterson Offers a Moving Story of One Man's Final Pilgrimage." *First Person Book Page*. www.bookpage.com/9904bp/david_guterson.html.

Murray, Donald M. "One Writer's Curriculum." *The English Journal* 80, no. 4 (1991): 16–20.

Nin, Anaïs. *The Diary of Anaïs Nin*, vol. 5. (1947–1955). Orlando, FL: Harvest/HBJ Books, 1975, 171.

Nisker, Wes. *The Essential Crazy Wisdom*. Berkeley, CA: Ten Speed Press, 2001.

Nordon, Pierre. *Conan Doyle*. Translated by Frances Partridge. London: John Murray, 1966.

Oates, Wayne E. *Nurturing Silence in a Noisy Heart*. Minneapolis, MN: Augsburg Fortress Publishers, 1996.

PBS Online. "The Martyrdoms of Saints Perpetua and Felicitas." *Frontline: From Jesus to Christ*. www.pbs.org/wghb/pages/frontline/shows/religion/maps/primary/perpetua.html.

———. "Transcript: Bill Moyers Interviews Isabel Allende." *NOW*. www.pbs.org/now/transcript/transcript_allende.html.

Perry, Susan K. *Writing in Flow: Keys to Enhanced Creativity*. Cincinnati, OH: Writer's Digest Books, 2001.

Plimpton, George. *The Writer's Chapbook: A Compendium of Fact, Opinion, Wit, and Advice from the Twentieth Century's Preeminent Writers*. New York: Viking, 1989.

"Questions Students Often Ask Elaine Marie Alphin." www.elainemariealphin.com/Alphin_FAQ.html.

Reynolds, Susan Salter. "'Our World' by Mary Oliver." *Los Angeles Times*, January 6, 2008. www.latimes.com/features/books/la-bk-reynolds6jan06,0,5486849.story.

Richards, Linda. "Clive Barker Comes Out: An Intimate Visit with One of the Masters of Scary Stuff." *January Magazine*. www.januarymagazine.com/barker.html.

———. "'G' Is for Grafton: Sue Grafton's Murderous Moments." *January Magazine*. www.januarymagazine.com/grafton.html.

Robertson-Lorant, Laurie. *Melville: A Biography*. New York: Clarkson-Potter, 1996.

Robinson, Maisah. "Gwendolyn Brooks: 1st African American to Receive Pulitzer Prize." *Suite 101*. www.suite101.com/article.cfm/african_american_history/60161.

Shelley, Percy Bysshe. "Defense of Poetry." *Modern History Sourcebook*. www.fordham.edu/halsall/mod/shelley-poetry.html.

Smith, Cynthia Leitich. "Rituals." *Cynsations*. July 14, 2004. www.cynthialeitichsmith.blogspot.com/2004/07/rituals.html.

St. Teresa of Avila. *Interior Castle, or The Mansions*. Edited by F. Benedict Zimmerman. Whitefish, MT: Kessenger Publishing, 2003.

Stocker, Michael. "Sound and the Subconscious." *Hear Where We Are.* Michael Stocker Associates. www.msa-design.com.

Turnbull, Andrew. *Scott Fitzgerald.* New York: Scribner's, 1962.

Vecchione, Patrice. *Writing and the Spiritual Life: Finding Your Voice by Looking Within.* Chicago: Contemporary Books, 2001.

Ventura, Michael. "The Talent of the Room." *LA Weekly* (May 1993): 22. www.laweekly.com.

Wendland, Ann. "The Next Thoreau: Place-Based Essays with the Power to Change Us." *The Exchange* (Winter 2004): 6–7.

White, E. B. "The Ring of Time." In *Modern American Prose*, edited by John Clifford and Robert DiYanni, 486–490. New York: McGraw Hill, 1993.

William Penn House. www.williampennhouse.org.

Woolf, Virginia. *A Room of One's Own.* Orlando, FL: Harcourt, 1991.

Wordsworth, William. "The Table Turned." www.poetryfoundation.org.

Worth Abbey. "Monasticism Today." www.worth.org.uk/guides/m8.

Zahara, Helen V. "The Placid Lake of the Mind." In *Approaches to Meditation*, edited by Virginia Hanson. Wheaton, IL: The Theosophical Publishing House, 1976.

INDEX